So Free!

So Free!

An In-Depth Guide to Deliverance and Inner Healing

William Sudduth

Chosen

Grand Rapids, Michigan

© 2007 by William Sudduth

Published by Chosen Books
a division of Baker Publishing Group
P.O. Box 6287, Grand Rapids, MI 49516-6287
www.chosenbooks.com

Printed in the United States of America

Library of Congress Cataloging-in-Publication Data
Sudduth, William, 1955–
    So free! : an in-depth guide to deliverance and inner healing / William Sudduth.
        p. cm.
    Includes bibliographical references and index.
    ISBN 10: 0-8007-9419-2 (pbk.)
    ISBN 978-0-8007-9419-4 (pbk.)
    1. Pastoral counseling. 2. Exorcism. 3. Spiritual healing. 4. Spiritual warfare. I. Title.
BV4012.2.S83 2007
234'.131—dc22   2006025713

The information given in *So Free!* is biblical, pastoral and spiritual in nature. It is not professional or medical counsel and should not be viewed as such. William Sudduth, RAM Ministries and Chosen Books hereby disclaim any and all responsibility or liability for any adverse or damaging effects that may be asserted or claimed to have arisen as a result of use of this material.

Contents

**Part 3   Ministering Deliverance and Inner
             Healing**

Foreword

Bill Sudduth is a wonderful personal friend and colleague who has labored in the trenches of deliverance with *great gifting, great skill* and *great spiritual power*. He is an uncomplicated person with a heart of gold, who found salvation and freedom as a mature adult. God did so much for him that his passion now is to help set others free from demonic spirits, much like those that once held him captive. He has "been there, done that," and understands the field of deliverance in biblical teaching, theory and practice.

Bill is a *great person* with a *great passion*, accompanied by a *great sense of humor*, and I vouch for his *great credibility*. We have taught together, and Bill teaches with the intensity of life and death being on the line. Deliverance *is* sometimes a case of life and death! We know that our enemy has come to "steal, kill and destroy," and that people chained in bondage and ignorance are his greatest treasure. Deliverance ministers love to snatch out of Satan's grip those people held in bondage and despair, and to set them free to be all God intended them to be. Bill himself is one such person.

I smiled when I read in his testimony that he had been an exterminator and pest controller as he was working his way through Bible school. I was a dairy farmer's daughter and loved the cows and other farm animals as I was growing up, working in the gardens and fields, especially running the tractors and harvesting equipment. I spent many hours doing what some "city slickers" would scorn—shoveling manure. That job had to be done daily in the wintertime, and it had to be done completely. You did not quit in the middle of cleaning the drop because you were tired or would rather be doing something else.

I believe God was preparing both Bill and me for deliverance ministry by giving us experience in going after the undesirable, smelly, unglamorous but satisfying feeling of a job carried to completion. A clean house that is free from pests is a nice house. We can then give tools to the former captives on how to keep that house in good condition.

Such tools are given in these pages. This material is refined and offered only after *great experience*.

Bill also presents this material with *great simplicity*. Deliverance ministry can be done by the rank and file of true believers in the pews with a little understanding and training. Jesus proclaimed this very thing in Mark 16:17–18: "These signs will follow those who believe: In My name they will cast out demons; they will speak with new tongues; they will take up serpents; and if they drink anything deadly, it will by no means hurt them; they will lay hands on the sick, and they will recover."

Bill shows people how to gain freedom and go out in turn and set others free. What a great service to the Body of Christ! It is not hard or spooky or difficult. It just takes a little faith and willingness; and with this simple, clear teaching, one can gain the confidence to be free and then to free others.

This book also contains *great research*, both biblical and practical. What is taught here is backed by Scripture as well as by *great experience*. It is a serious attempt to share knowledge and experience to give others a leg up in this ministry. You yourself can build on this *great foundation*!

The practical questionnaires and prayers of confession and renunciation are a *great help and guide* to get you started, either in becoming free or in helping to free others. Bill provides lots of suggestions for a wide variety of possible circumstances that might arise. (We have discovered, however, that Satan does not invent a whole lot that is new.) Much of what we might encounter will be here somewhere. The chapter entitled "Deliverance: The End-Time Ministry" is outstanding and worth the price of the book!

As I have worked in the field of deliverance for about 25 years now, my heart is warmed to see younger choice servants help swell the ranks of deliverance ministers and equippers. Believe me, there is no more grateful a person on planet earth than one who has been set free from demonic oppression. I know it is in that spirit that Bill has painstakingly written this book, both in gratitude to God and as one of His instruments to help equip God's people to minister to others.

You hold in your hands a *great tool*, written lovingly to help others. My prayer is that God will cause this tool to have *great exposure* and will cause it to blossom in many hearts and lives.

Doris M. Wagner
Cofounder, International Society of Deliverance Ministers
Coordinator of the Deliverance Concentration,
Wagner Leadership Institute
Executive vice president, Global Harvest Ministries
Colorado Springs, Colorado
June 2006

Introduction

"My people are destroyed [or perish] from lack of knowledge."

Hosea 4:6, NIV

As I woke up one morning, the Lord was speaking to me. Actually, He spoke through me as I awakened. He said, *My people are still perishing from a lack of knowledge.* It is my desire to share with you some of the knowledge, the wisdom, the insight and the understanding needed to walk in victory, and, in turn, to help others do the same. I want to make you aware of the wiles and schemes of the devil—how to recognize them and how to overcome them.

We often say, "Jesus loves you and has a plan for your life." Well, I want you to know that the devil, Satan, hates you, and he has a plan for your life as well. His plan is to steal your joy and peace, and to kill you, if at all possible. If he cannot kill you, he will do everything in his power to destroy you, your family, your church, your ministry, your anointing and your witness. Through the ministry of deliverance, the plans of the enemy can be recognized, avoided and overcome, thus freeing us to walk fully in God's plan for our lives.

The ministry of deliverance is a miracle and nothing less. Seeing someone who has been bound with demonic bondage from his past and the sins of his ancestors become totally and marvelously set free is a tremendously rewarding and exciting experience. The fact that I am writing a book is also an absolute miracle.

When I was a young child, my aunt Janet took me to Sunday school at a Presbyterian church in Maryland. In 1968, when I was in the sixth grade, I was confirmed. I recited the Apostles' Creed from memory and was added to the membership of the church. Sadly, that same year I was also introduced to the drug culture by a classmate. His older brother had come home from college and turned him on to speed. He then sent my friend to school with the drug in order to make converts.

At that point I made a decision. I chose the things of this world and decided to forsake the things of God. By the time I reached high school, I was heavily addicted to amphetamines and was dealing drugs to support my own habit. I was a speed freak who drank heavily to take the edge off the speed. I spent the next 28 years wreaking havoc in my own life and the lives of everyone around me. I was searching to fill a void in my life that could not be filled with drugs, alcohol, sex or achievements.

As I am writing this book, I am seeing firsthand the power of God in my life. The ability He has given me to write this book is amazing to me. Every day I am reminded of the awesome delivering power of Jesus Christ and how He set me free from the addictions, bondage and strongholds in my life.

I have the privilege of watching His manifest power unfold daily, not only in my life, but also in the lives of others as He sets them free from their own strongholds. It is awesome to see what God can and will do with our lives, if only we will surrender to Him and obey Him.

I want to give Him all the glory for this work and everything else He has done in my life. I would not and could not have undertaken this task without His grace or His hand on my life. A verse of Scripture comes to mind: "When they saw the courage of Peter and John and realized that they were unschooled, ordinary men, they were astonished and they took note that these men had been with Jesus" (Acts 4:13, NIV).

Folks, I, too, have been with Jesus. He has become real to me, and His Word has become alive to me. Most people tend to think that someone who casts out demons is somehow super-spiritual or hyper-spiritual, having supernatural insight into the spirit realm. I do not believe myself to be super- or hyper-spiritual because I minister in this area. I believe that my childlike faith and trust in God, combined with my bulldog tenacity, have been the keys to my ministry success.

Deliverance is a lot more than just casting out demons. It is a ministry that deals with people's hurts and wounds and all the junk they carry from the past. Deliverance ministry most often involves a combination of counseling, inner healing and deliverance. In essence, it means simply (1) listening to the Holy Spirit in order to hear what He has to say from the Word of God about the person's needs and problems, and (2) ministering that truth to the person.

I have found the Word of God to be the most powerful weapon in the area of deliverance. I believe every word in the Bible is true, and I also believe it is for today. When the Word of God is ministered with effectiveness and power, hell cannot stand against it. The Word is truth, and the truth sets you free! How free? *So free!*

I would like to give thanks to everyone who helped put this book together. I could not have done this on my own. The local body of Christ was truly involved. A special thanks to my wife, Janet, and my daughter, Robyn, for their patience with me as I worked late into the night to finish it. Thanks to Elisha French, Shelly McWilliams, Eva Koelner, Jim and Patsy Shreve, Josh Fisher and all the others who helped me research, compile data and edit the book. I would also like to thank all the men and women of God who poured themselves into me these last ten years. This is also the fruit of your labor!

Part 1

On Deliverance

One

Deliverance: The End-Time Ministry

The Church is experiencing a significant upswing of interest in the subject of deliverance. New ministries are popping up all around us. Reference books and teaching manuals cover the shelves. Magazines probe the subject. Seminars and conferences relating to deliverance ministry abound. I know of television and radio programs that have actually aired deliverance sessions.

Just a few decades ago, only certain charismatic sectors of the Church were intent on understanding this ministry, but today many parts of the Body are involved. Roman Catholic, Protestant mainline and nondenominational churches are joining with charismatic congregations to acknowledge the reality of demonic oppression.

I remember reading several years ago, for instance, that the Vatican had produced its first updated ritual for exorcism since 1614.[1] Even the pope himself has been called upon to deal with deliverance issues. Pope John Paul II was imparting a blessing in a general audience once when he was confronted by

> a pretty nineteen-year-old girl from a small town near Monza, Italy, who began to shout uncontrollably. Italian police immediately came to the scene and tried to calm her. However, she showed superhuman strength and was able to repel the police. She shouted meaningless phrases in a cavernous voice . . . the girl literally "vomited" insults at the Bishop Gianni Danzi. Pope John Paul II met the possessed girl in a separate area. He exorcised her and prayed for her for half an hour. He then promised to offer his Mass the following day for her, so that she would be released from her possession.[2]

Father Gabriele Amorth is the official exorcist of the Vatican and has performed thousands of exorcisms. He had worked with this same girl prior to the Pope's audience and again after the Pope prayed with her. However, his attempts to exorcise her proved futile. In fact, the demon taunted him, saying, "Your boss (the Pope) could not get me out either." According to Father Amorth, "It was a severe case of demon possession and the girl was suffering from the results of a curse."[3]

And there is this story about globally acclaimed minister of charity Mother Teresa:

> The Archbishop of Calcutta has admitted that in the months prior to Mother Teresa's death in 1997 at the age of eighty-seven, he ordered an exorcism performed on her because of fears she was being attacked by the devil. When the nun who devoted her life to caring for the poorest of the poor in Calcutta's worst slums was having trouble sleeping, the archbishop diagnosed the insomnia as the devil's work. "When doctors said they could not find a medical reason for her sleeplessness, I thought she might be getting attacked by the devil," Archbishop Henry Sebastian D'Souza told Reuters. "I wanted her to calm down and asked a priest, in

the name of the Church, to perform an exorcism prayer on her. She happily agreed." The exorcism—which is the casting out of an evil spirit through prayer—took about thirty minutes. It was performed by the Rev. Rosario Stroscio, a seventy-nine-year-old priest who was born in Sicily but has lived in Calcutta for sixty-two years. He told Reuters, "She was a little dazed and behaved strangely. Maybe Mother Teresa was under harassment from Satan, but after the prayers, she was quite calm." Mother Teresa was able to sleep following the ancient ritual. "After he performed these prayers, she slept very well that night," the archbishop said. Mother Teresa, who won a Nobel Prize, founded the Missionaries of Charity and is on the fast track to sainthood. "Since she was such a holy person, the devil could [have been] tempted to attack her," D'Souza explained.[4]

The accelerated interest in the supernatural is not just a focus of the religious world. Fascination with the demonic has infiltrated the secular world as well. As a modern turning point we might note the rerelease of the popular movie *The Exorcist*. This movie, which chronicles a Catholic priest's battle over a demon-possessed girl, was originally released in 1973. The 1970s marked a significant upswing in deliverance ministry. The movie's rerelease in September 2000 coincided with the renewed focus that we are witnessing today.

Several months after the second release of the movie and its attendant fascination with the work of the devil, a national conference of Roman Catholic bishops issued a statement expressing concern about the "unhealthy interest" being awakened in the occult through media exposure. It noted a rebirth of divinations, fortune-telling, witchcraft and black magic, often combined with a superstitious use of religion.

This kind of parallel activity is not just happenstance; secular interest in the occult gives the devil great opportunity to deceive. I believe the same devil has the same wiles and the same schemes today as he had two thousand years ago. He is constantly trying to counterfeit God's work in an attempt to disprove it.

Spiraling Down

A few years ago I attended a deliverance crusade led by Argentine evangelist Carlos Annacondia. Brother Annacondia ministers all over the world. This particular conference was held in Orlando, Florida, with about four thousand people in attendance each night.

I am sure some unsaved people were there, but for the most part Christians were in attendance. I was surprised, then, to see about a thousand people go forward each night for the altar call. In response Brother Annacondia proceeded to provoke the devil by commanding evil spirits to come out. People all over the auditorium started shrieking and screaming as the presence of demons was manifested. When this happened, they were ushered out to the deliverance room where teams from local churches, who had been trained by the crusade directors prior to the event, ministered to them.

I was overwhelmed by the large number of Christians who were "manifesting" and I asked God about it. *Lord*, I said, *these cannot all be unsaved people who are manifesting.*

He took me to this parable in Luke 14:16–24:

> Then [Jesus said], "A certain man gave a great supper and invited many, and sent his servant at supper time to say to those who were invited, 'Come, for all things are now ready.' But they all with one accord began to make excuses. The first said to him, 'I have bought a piece of ground, and I must go and see it. I ask you to have me excused.' And another said, 'I have bought five yoke of oxen, and I am going to test them. I ask you to have me excused.' Still another said, 'I have married a wife, and therefore I cannot

come.' So that servant came and reported these things to his master. Then the master of the house, being angry, said to his servant, 'Go out quickly into the streets and lanes of the city, and bring in here the poor and the maimed and the lame and the blind.' And the servant said, 'Master, it is done as you commanded, and still there is room.' Then the master said to the servant, 'Go out into the highways and hedges, and compel them to come in, that my house may be filled. For I say to you that none of those men who were invited shall taste my supper.'"

The Lord then said to me, *The highways and hedges are the gutter.* He was pulling these people out of the gutter, just as He had with me.

I am convinced that we are going to see Him do a lot more of this as our world goes deeper into darkness.

You have no doubt heard some of the statistics that show how bruised and broken and needy our world is. Particularly startling are statistics that relate to the coming generations. As the children from Generation X have grown to adulthood and Generation Y or so-called "Millennials" have followed in their footsteps, we are seeing staggering numbers of hurt, abused, abandoned, rejected, messed-up people.

More and more children are coming from broken homes: The divorce rate among believers is equal to that of nonbelievers—more than 60 percent. Outreach groups like Teen Mania report that 48 percent of high school seniors are sexually active; 91 percent believe that there is "no absolute truth"; 58 percent of teens have viewed objectionable content on the Internet.[5] The American Academy of Pediatrics reports that children in the United States watch about four hours of television every day. These children tend to be overweight because they are not running and playing and getting the exercise they need, and because commercials trigger the desire for unhealthy food. Hundreds of studies have shown that the thousands upon thousands of hours that children watch television can make them immune to the horror of violence and accept it as a way to solve problems in real life: They will see about *eight thousand* murders on television before they finish grade school.[6] And the computerized games young people play are proving to be deadly.

Several years ago my stepfather had a massive stroke. I flew home to be with him and my family. While I was there, my mother expressed concern about my nephew who was living with her and my stepfather at that time. She said that he spent countless hours on the computer and television playing video games.

One evening I made it a point to visit him and see what he was up to. I talked with him about the Lord, and he assured me he was a Christian and was in a right relationship with the Lord. I then asked him, "If that is the case, why do you have all these books on witchcraft, vampires and the occult?" He assured me that he did not really read them that much anymore. I explained to him how having demonic junk in our homes gives demons squatter's rights and suggested he get rid of it. My nephew agreed and we started going through his things.

You may recall the game Dungeons & Dragons, which has been around for some thirty years. My nephew was deeply involved in the game and had written notes that described in great detail how to commit a murder. He had thought through the ways of obtaining the murder weapon, how and when to commit the murder, and how to dispose of the body. I was shocked. My nephew explained that this was part of the game. You were required to plot a perfect murder in order to play. I was totally amazed by this game and how demonic and deceiving it was.

And games have only gotten more sophisticated. Modern role-playing games use stunning real-life technology to draw players deeper and deeper into demonic deception. In November 2005 the National Institute on Media and the

Family (NIMF) released its tenth MediaWise Video and Computer Game Report Card. Here is a portion of that report:

Every child who plays video games is undergoing a powerful developmental experiment, the results of which we do not yet fully comprehend. . . . In early July, we discovered that explicit pornography was included in the top selling video game, Grand Theft Auto: San Andreas. . . . The ESRB video game rating system, like its cousins in the movie and television industries, is owned and operated by the industry it is supposed to monitor. This obvious conflict of interest is why only eighteen games out of ten thousand have ever been rated Adults Only (AO). It seems that every year M-rated games are on average more violent, contain more sexual content and have more profane language than games released with the same rating the year before. Study after study shows that ratings would be stricter if parents were doing the job. It took explicit porn to get Grand Theft Auto: San Andreas an AO rating, even though the original version, still rated M, rewards players whose onscreen persona had sex with prostitutes and then killed them.[7]

A survey by the NIMF found that 87 percent of eight- to seventeen-year-old children play video games at home. And parents are not monitoring the games they play. Only about a quarter of the children surveyed stated that their parents have stopped them from purchasing a video game based on its rating.[8]

The Internet is another powerful tool that Satan is using to deepen America's dysfunction and sink her deeper into the gutter. One way is by giving unlimited access to pornography. I have read that one-third of all Internet hits download pornography. There are more than a million pornographic pictures on the Internet, and fifteen hundred new pornographic sites are added to the World Wide Web each week. The National Council for Missing and Exploited Children (NCMEC) reports that child pornography on the Internet is a multibillion-dollar business. "Not only have we seen an increase in reports of Internet child pornography, but the victims are becoming younger and the images are becoming more graphic and violent," reports NCMEC president Ernie Allen.[9]

Another way that Satan reaches people through the Internet is by preying on their loneliness. I believe that loneliness is the number one problem in America. People feel abandoned and rejected and just want to talk with someone who cares about them. Sadly, the Church is falling short in fulfilling that need, so the devil uses chat rooms to meet it. And not just secular chat rooms: I cannot tell you of all the people our ministry (Righteous Acts Ministries, Inc.) has prayed with who got into a mess while in a Christian chat room. A lonely Christian girl goes into a chat room one day, and the next day she is in another state with a man she does not know.

Not long ago my wife, Janet, and I were holding revival meetings at a church in New York. The pastor asked us to meet with a girl from his congregation and the boy she had met through a chat room on the Internet. The boy was from Canada and had flown in to meet her and her parents. He now wanted her to fly back to Canada with him to meet his parents. The pastor was concerned for one of his sheep, and with good reason. We talked to this couple and I agreed with the pastor; I questioned this boy's motives.

Several nights later in a revival meeting the boy came to the altar and got saved. He then went to the girl's father and confessed that he had come under false pretenses. He called his family in Canada and confessed his sins to them. The next day he flew home.

What if God had not intervened in this matter? What would have become of this godly but lonely young lady? This man she met in a Christian chat room was not a believer, and she almost left the country with him. You have no idea whom you are chatting with. Satan himself could be on that other keyboard. I know of other similar incidents that did not have good endings.

I remember one such story about a fifteen-year-old girl who met a man on the Internet. She made the mistake of meeting with him. He kidnapped her and prostituted her to two other men as a sex slave. She managed to escape, and the men were arrested. They were charged with kidnapping, rape and sodomy. I am sure this young girl needed extensive counseling, inner healing and deliverance—just one of many, many cases that show the crisis we have reached in the world today.

Making Our Move

Are you getting the picture? A cosmic struggle is unfolding before our very eyes. On the one hand the devil is moving with the end-time fury promised in Revelation 12:12; our society is spiraling toward hell. On the other hand, God is bringing the ministry of deliverance to the forefront once again and pulling untold numbers out of the gutter. As the coming generations get saved, there will be a lot of messes to clean up. Deliverance is truly the end-time ministry.

One night I had a dream that helped me understand this. I was positioned on a chessboard. The pieces around me were ornate and larger than life. I then realized that I was one of the pieces: a pawn. So I looked to see who was playing the game.

Looking up and over the pieces behind me, I saw the Ancient of Days sitting on a throne, leaning over the board. With His hand on His chin, He was pondering the next move. I was awestruck because I knew it was God. Looking to the opposite side I was surprised to see His opponent. I knew it was Satan, although he did not have horns or a

pointed tail as I had expected. As I looked at both oppo-
nents, I realized they were looking at me! I saw that they
were both waiting for me to make a move, and that neither
of them could move until I did. My move would determine
which one of them would move next.

Wow! Here I was, a pawn in the middle of a cosmic game
of strategy, and I had the power to affect the outcome. You
also have that same power! We each have control over our
own destinies. Everything we do has a natural and a spiritual consequence. As this cosmic battle continues, we need
to be ever seeking the Father's heart and moving according
to His Spirit. He, in turn, will move on our behalf.

One day, as I pondered this awesome responsibility, I
had a vision of Satan sitting in his living room, watching
his favorite soap opera on television. I pictured him kicked
back in a recliner with the remote in his hand. Suddenly a
loud ruckus began outside his door. He turned and looked
out the window to see a bunch of Christians standing there,
binding, loosing, rebuking and reviling him. Satan looked
at them, waved his hand and said, "Ha!" He then went
right back to watching his soap opera. Sadly, I believe this
is the extent of the damage most folks do to the kingdom
of hell.

Next I pictured a Christian kicking in the devil's front
door, walking over to his television, picking it up, yanking
the plug out of the wall and heading for the door. At this
point the devil, filled with fury, jumped out of his recliner
and a knockdown, drag-out fight ensued.

You see, it is one thing to talk and sing about deliverance,
but it is a whole different matter to start plundering hell
and actually taking back what the enemy has stolen from
us. When you enter into the deliverance ministry, you enter
into true spiritual warfare.

Let me be quick to add, however, that we are not seeking
formulas. Formulas are not what set people free. What sets
people free is the delivering power of Jesus Christ through

His Holy Spirit. I truly believe that God often sets His children free in spite of our feeble attempts to understand the spirit realm and our limited knowledge of exorcism or deliverance! The important thing is hearing what God has to say about the individuals' problems and ministering that truth to them.

Remember the parable of the talents found in Matthew 25:14–30? The master gave one servant five talents, one servant two talents and to another he gave one talent. He then held them accountable for those talents. I find it interesting that the word *talent* meant coinage in Jesus' time, and now it describes abilities or gifting.

I believe we will be held accountable for how we use the talents God has given us (or should I say, entrusted to us). Whether we are considering finances, skills, revealed truths, knowledge or anointing, God expects us to be good stewards of all that He provides. He does not want us to blow it.

We, as the Church, need to know that Jesus Christ is coming back and He is coming back soon. Furthermore He is coming back for a Bride—a pure, spotless, unblemished, unwrinkled and undefiled Bride, not a Bride who is all bound up in sin, shame or the things of this world. God is giving the Church another opportunity to flow in this ministry of deliverance as a part of our preparation.

But this will not happen without conflict. And as we will discover in the next chapter, the main conflict about deliverance ministry seems to come from the Church herself. Can a Christian have a demon? It is a question that brings sharp division. Let's explore the answer.

Two

Can a Christian Be "Possessed"?

As interest in deliverance ministry rises, so does the controversy surrounding it. Because of past abuses occurring in the deliverance ministry—notably in the 1970s and early 1980s—many churches and leaders have a bad taste in their mouths for deliverance. In those days people were casting demons out of everyone and everything, including hymnals, pews, fingernail polish and hairdos! The Church is still sharply divided on the subject of deliverance.

Along with the Church's own uncertainty about this ministry, Satan is doing whatever he can to discredit it and to further the discord and confusion in the Body of Christ. He cannot stop God from bringing deliverance ministry into the frontlines, of course, but he can try to subvert it with abuses and extremes. To tell you the truth, Satan really does not have to work too hard for people to slip into the extreme way of doing things. People tend to go to extremes with or without the devil's help. I am certain there are times when Satan stands before God, shakes his head and says rightly, "I had nothing to do with that."

In the ministry of deliverance, as with all biblical pursuits, there is a central point of truth. The problem is that we as humans have a hard time staying centered. We are like a pendulum that swings in opposite directions. As we swing this way and that, a little bit of truth goes along for the ride and seems to give credence to ideas on either side that are really extreme views.

This is similar to what happened with the Faith Movement in years past. God brought that truth—the relationship between faith and answered prayer—to light, but people pushed it to extremes and misused it. The abuses that surfaced in the Faith Movement (especially those regarding wealth and prosperity) have left many people afraid to talk or preach about prosperity or money. Even worse, the abuses have caused many people to equate Christianity with prosperity, which is not truth. Christianity is about salvation and souls. It is about Christ and Him crucified. It is about His people being set free; it is not about money.

And now misguided teaching about the deliverance ministry is leading to the same kind of misuse. In this case, one side declares, to use a well-worn phrase, that there is a demon behind every rock. I often comment on this view by joking, "The more I am involved in this deliverance ministry, the less I believe there is a demon behind every rock. No, I think there are *two* of them."

The other side denies demonic activity altogether. It claims that everything that happens is a product of the flesh. If something goes wrong in a person's life, this side responds with either "You are not saved" or "You have no faith." It is not unusual for these individuals to lean toward the cessationist belief that the gifts of the Spirit, as well as the need for these gifts, passed away with the last apostle.

Personally I think that both of these extremes are incorrect; the truth is somewhere in the middle. I would say this: *Many born-again believers walk in the flesh and not in the spirit. By doing so, they open doors for the enemy to attack them and gain ground in their lives.*

Now it is also true that whenever we resist these two extremes by living in the Spirit, we usually come into personal confrontation with the enemy. New levels bring about new devils as the old saying goes. But that is different from opening a door for the enemy to come in and make himself at home.

Author Graham Cooke gives interesting insight about the struggle between flesh and spirit: "The enemy doesn't have the time or manpower (demon power) to afflict every Christian personally. He mostly uses the flesh and the world to keep us out of God's will."[1]

Walking in the flesh is our choice. The apostle Paul wrote this about the operation of the flesh:

> Now the works of the flesh are evident, which are: adultery, fornication, uncleanness, lewdness, idolatry, sorcery, hatred, contentions, jealousies, outbursts of wrath, selfish ambitions, dissensions, heresies, envy, murders, drunkenness, revelries, and the like; of which I tell you beforehand, just as I also told you in time past, that those who practice such things will not inherit the kingdom of God.
>
> Galatians 5:19–21

All of these works of the flesh act just like open doors: They allow the devil to come and attack. It is in this regard that Paul also warned us not to give the devil any footholds in our lives:

> Therefore, putting away lying, "Let each one of you speak truth with his neighbor," for we are members of one another. "Be angry, and do not sin": do not let the sun go down on your wrath, nor give place to the devil.
>
> Ephesians 4:25–27

Why would the apostle write to "give no place to the devil" unless there was a place you could give him? The word used here for "place" is the Greek word *topos*. It is the word from which we get the English word *topography*. Topography is the study and mapping of land. This Scripture is actually saying to us, "Do not give the devil a piece of ground to stand on in your life. Do not give him a foothold or he will create a stronghold."

Teresa Castleman, who was head of personal ministry at Brownsville Assembly of God in Pensacola, Florida, for several years explains it this way: "Picture a 160-acre estate with a big iron fence, concrete pillars and a big iron gate. One day the owner goes to town and leaves the gate open. A passerby sees the nice house, big fence and an open gate, so he enters. No one challenges him. He then heads to the south forty and pitches a tent."

Now let me ask you. Does the passerby have a legal right to set up residence? Of course not. But is he there? Yes, he is. Why is he there? Simply because of the open gate or open door. You see, because of the open doors in our lives Satan comes in and establishes footholds. Those footholds soon become strongholds.

Possession versus Control

Now, let's look at the real controversy, the real question, the real argument that has the Church so sharply divided: Can a Christian have a demon? I have heard this question answered quite sensibly: "Who wants one?" Now that is a great response, but it does not really answer the question, does it? Personally I believe a Christian can have anything he or she wants.

The question we should ask, therefore, is this: Can a Christian be demon-possessed? In order to answer this, we must first look at the meaning of the word *possession*. Possession indicates total control or ownership.

Let me share with you an example that I first heard from Pastor Cary Robertson when he was associate pastor of Brownsville Assembly of God. He explained it this way: "I own a Ford Taurus automobile. It is paid for, and I have the title to it. Now, you can go to my home and slash my tires, scratch the paint and break all of the windows. You could even take it out on a joy ride. You cannot, however, legally sell it or trade it in because I hold the title to it. I own it."

Similarly all Christians, even disobedient ones, belong to God and not to Satan. Scripture says, "For you were bought at a price; therefore glorify God in your body and in your spirit, *which are God's*" (1 Corinthians 6:20, emphasis added).

Whose? God's! First Corinthians 7:23 states again, "You were bought at a price." Paul repeated what he had said earlier because he wanted it to be crystal clear.

Ephesians 1:14 further speaks about our belonging to God. The Holy Spirit "is the guarantee of our inheritance until the redemption of the *purchased possession*" (emphasis added). The New International Version states it this way: The Holy Spirit "is a deposit guaranteeing our inheritance until the redemption of those who are *God's possession*—to the praise of his glory" (emphasis added).

God owns you and me. Period! Satan cannot possess us because we are a purchased possession. God holds the "title" to us. Besides, I do not believe that Satan wants to possess us. Satan is content just to keep us in bondage in some area of our lives. He is happy scratching the paint and smashing a few windows in our lives, to use the car analogy, in order to cause us to stumble and fall or simply to keep us from fulfilling God's plan for our lives. (You probably know that there are a lot of Christians out there running on flat tires and all beaten up.)

The book of Acts tells the story of Simon the Sorcerer. This is a good example of a Christian, or at least a believer, in bondage. Simon believed, he was baptized and he followed after Philip (see Acts 8:13). Simon was amazed by the things of God, yet he was full of junk, bound by sin and full of bitterness.

I have heard this Scripture used for two arguments. Some people use it to show that Christians can indeed have bondages in their lives. Other people say that Simon's conversion was not genuine because his heart was not right with God. I am not going to try to determine the validity of Simon's conversion.

My question is, How many people do we have in our churches today who fit this very same description? There are people who have believed and have been baptized, yet they are sitting in our churches full of junk, bound by sin and full of bitterness.

Are they saved? Are their hearts right with God? Only God knows the condition of people's hearts, unless we are given a divine revelation such as Peter had with Simon. Are they Christians or just believers? *Christian* means to be Christlike. How many people do you know who are truly Christlike?

James wrote, "You believe that there is one God. You do well. Even the demons believe—and tremble!" (James 2:19). There are a lot of believers in our churches today who do not tremble. They have no fear of the Lord and no reverence for the things of God. Are believers without fear of or reverence for the Lord Christlike? Are they truly Christians? Are they even saved? These are good questions, and I do not have the answers! I do know, however, that during my experience as an usher at Brownsville Assembly of God, I encountered numerous people from all around this nation and the world. Many of them who claimed to be Christians showed less reverence for God and His house than I did as a total heathen.

The point is, a believer is the Lord's possession, but the devil can still make a mess of that person's life. Janet and I have both worked in the deliverance ministry for numerous years. We have ministered in individual settings and in large group deliverance settings with Cleansing Stream Ministries (a deliverance and inner healing ministry offered through The Church On The Way in Van Nuys, California) and other types of deliverance seminars. In our experience, we have found that Christians, even though they cannot be demon-possessed, can certainly be oppressed by the devil.

Acts speaks of Jesus' ministry to all who were oppressed: "how God anointed Jesus of Nazareth with the Holy Spirit and with power, who went about doing good and healing all who were *oppressed by the devil*, for God was with Him" (Acts 10:38, emphasis added).

The Greek word *daimonizoma* is translated in the King James Version as "possessed," but this is a poor translation of that word. It would be better translated as "to have a demon" or "to be under the power of or the influence of a demon" or "to be demonized." I often use this word *demonized*. By it I mean that *Satan, through his demons, can exercise direct partial control in an area or areas of a Christian's life.* Now you may not agree with this, but if you do not, then explain why we have so much hell in our churches, in our marriages, in our homes and in our own lives!

A Demonically Oppressed Christian

A few years ago Janet and I went on a missions trip to the inner city of Cancun, Mexico, with a group from the Brownsville Revival School of Ministry (BRSM). The first night we were there, as well as every night, the anointing was thick during the praise and worship. The manifest presence of God was felt strongly.

That first night Janet noticed a Mexican woman who, as the anointing increased, backed slowly out of the room where the service was being held. We had an incredible night. God moved and the people were touched mightily. After the service Janet told me about the Mexican woman she had seen. She wanted me to find out if we could minister to this woman in the area of deliverance if she came to the meeting the following night. I assured her I would ask permission from the trip leader as well as the pastor of the church. The next morning I received permission from both leaders, and we prayed that God would bring her to the meeting that night.

That evening the woman returned. As the praise and worship intensified, we watched as she again backed out of the service. At the prayer time, my wife sought her out and got an interpreter in an effort to talk and minister to her. I spotted Janet with the woman and noticed that the woman was starting to manifest. I proceeded to walk over to assist. I asked the interpreter if the girl spoke any English at all. He assured me that she spoke no English.

Janet continued to minister to this woman for a few minutes. Then I leaned over and said, "You foul spirit"— and that was all I got out of my mouth. The woman was thrown violently to the floor and began to curse me in flawless English. The voice, obviously not her own, told me that I had no authority there, that I had no power and no rights, and that this woman belonged to him, meaning the demon.

A crowd gathered instantly. Not wanting to embarrass her, we bound the spirit and took her to a back room to work with her. We took the interpreter with us and asked him to try to obtain some information about her background. (An interesting note: The interpreter told the demon to go back to hell where it belonged. The demon rebuked him and explained to us that the interpreter had no right to send it to hell before its appointed time.)

We spent several hours with the woman that evening and asked her husband—who, it turned out, was the worship leader—if he would bring her back. He agreed, and we met them the next morning with a small team that we had assembled. We ministered most of the day with little success. As we prayed, the demon cursed, rebuked and reviled us; we could not get very far.

Finally we asked her husband if he could shed any light on the situation. Her husband spoke with her a few minutes. He then told us that when she was a small child, her father, who was a Christian, left her mother for another woman. Her mother took the abandonment very hard and fell into deep depression. This little girl, watching her mother deteriorating rapidly, prayed and asked the demon that was tormenting her mother to stop tormenting her mother and come into her. The spirit obliged her by leaving her mother and entering her. Because of this specific invitation, the spirit now had a legal right to torment her, even years later as an adult.

With this new information, we proceeded. We used the interpreter and her husband to explain to the woman that she had to repent for allowing the demon to come into her. She also had to renounce and rebuke the demon, and break its power in her life. Once this was done, we then would be able to cast it out. She understood and agreed gladly to repent. As soon as she started to pray, however, she went into a zombie-like state. We began to bind the zombie spirit, but because it would not be bound we again asked her husband to help us.

Her husband began to sing a beautiful song. As he sang, we noticed a tear well up in her eye and roll down her cheek. She "came back" to us. It was an amazing sight. She started to do as we had instructed her—repent, renounce, rebuke and break the hold this demon had on her—but once more she fell into the trance-like state. Her husband sang again and we repeated that scenario over and over again. This went on for what seemed like hours.

All of a sudden my wife exclaimed, "Wait a minute! A husband can break a rash vow made by his wife." We asked her husband to repent for his wife, renounce and rebuke Satan and his demons, and break the curse his wife had spoken over herself.

As he prayed, his wife came out of the trance and spoke to him in English, saying, "I am going to kill you."

Her husband replied, "What did I do to you?"

The demon stated, "You took her from me."

We then commanded the demon to leave and it left with a shriek.

During the course of this session, we had discovered the name of the demon spirit was "Momma." Once that spirit was cast out, we began to deal with a second demon named "Death." We had a difficult time with this demon, but it was nothing like the first one because the woman had not given Death an invitation. The spirit tried several ploys with us. At one point it said to my wife, "I will leave if you will let me come into you." My wife rebuked the demon. At another time the spirit said, "I will leave in three days." We asked why it would leave in three days. It replied, "Because I am going to kill her in three days." We rebuked the demon.

Some time later, the demon finally said, "Okay, okay, I will leave. Stand back." Not thinking and being exhausted, we all stood back. The woman then jumped up and darted toward the open, second-story window. We tackled her to the ground, got her back into the chair and proceeded with the session. The spirit asked to be allowed to go into an animal. My weary wife replied, "You can go into a dog for all I care." The spirit left immediately, and the deliverance was complete. (Please note: We do not make it a practice of sending spirits into animals. Nor do we try to send them to hell or to the pit. We believe Scripture indicates that when they leave a person they go to a dry and arid place. See Matthew 12:43–45.)

We had spent a total of fifteen hours with this woman. When we gave her back to her husband, she was totally set free. The next morning we were astonished to see a large dog lying dead on the sidewalk in front of the church, in the exact place she would have landed had she been successful in jumping.

The next night, after her deliverance, this woman stood in the front of her church and testified to what the Lord had done. She told the congregation members and guests the whole story of how she had become demonized as a child. She told how the anointing of God had provoked the demons, and how Jesus Christ had set her free. She also stated that she had been a Christian for ten years and a worship leader's wife for eight years, and even though she had been demonized all those years, she had been producing "good fruit" in her life and in her ministry with her husband. Jesus taught that every tree is judged by its fruit. A good tree produces good fruit and a bad tree produces bad fruit.

About a year after this incident, I ran into the missionary's wife who had invited us to minister with the inner-city organization. She told me that this Mexican woman and her husband were traveling around the Yucatan Peninsula, going from church to church testifying about what had happened to her and how Jesus had set her free.

A Deeper Question

Was this woman saved? Was she a Christian? I believe she was both; she had accepted Jesus as her Lord and Savior and she was bearing fruit in keeping with her repentance. Yet was she demonized? There is no question that she was.

One day as I was praying about this the Lord reminded me of a cork that I had had years before in my tackle box. I recalled how fishing had been slow one day, so I had decided to clean up my tackle box. I had gathered all the loose hooks together. Then I had put all of the long-shanked hooks in one end of the cork, all of the short hooks in the other end and all of the odd-shaped hooks around the middle of the cork. That cork was stuck by hooks of various shapes and sizes from top to bottom. Then the Lord said to me, *This is what My people look like!*

If you have ever been snagged by a fishhook, you know how it hurts. The size of the fishhook does not matter; large or small, they all inflict pain and will cause damage. It is the same with "spiritual" hooks: Anger, jealousy, lust, greed, pride, perversion, etc., are wounding us in spirit, soul and body. We might well reword 2 Corinthians 10:4 to read like this: "For the weapons of our warfare are not carnal but mighty in God for pulling down strongholds and pulling out hooks"!

Until those hooks are removed, until the person is set free, Satan will continue to oppress whomever he can, Christian or not. He will continue to exert power over individuals and try to block them from moving in the fullness of the Holy Spirit.

Following Jesus

I explained at the opening of this chapter that the Church is divided about this ministry of deliverance; that pendulum of extreme teaching swings widely. But consider this: As much as one-third of Jesus' earthly ministry involved deliverance and healing. Here are just two examples from Scripture:

> And Jesus went about all Galilee, teaching in their synagogues, preaching the gospel of the kingdom, and healing all kinds of sickness and all kinds of disease among the people. Then His fame went throughout all Syria; and they brought to Him all sick people who were afflicted

with various diseases and torments, and those who were demon-possessed, epileptics, and paralytics; and He healed them.

Matthew 4:23–24

When evening had come, they brought to Him many who were demon-possessed. And He cast out the spirits with a word, and healed all who were sick.

Matthew 8:16

Jesus spent a major portion of His public ministry working in the area of deliverance. Should we as His followers expect our ministry to be any different?

In addition, Jesus' ministry was not without opposition. Surprisingly, the opposition He received was not from heathens or pagans, but from the religious leaders of His day. In Matthew 9:34 and Mark 3:22, the scribes and Pharisees accused Jesus of casting out demons by Beelzebub, the ruler of demons. They then accused Jesus of being demon-possessed. This was all because He was casting out demons.

You will find that it is certainly no different today! We, too, can and should expect the same type of resistance to this ministry. People *always* attack what they do not understand, and, trust me, people do not understand the ministry of deliverance. Not only that, but when you start plundering hell and setting people free, you are going to tick the devil off. So be prepared. The enemy will use anyone he has any influence on or control over to attack you or to discredit you and your ministry.

The controversy and opposition will no doubt continue, but you can be free and help others be free. This happens through our authority in Christ. Let's look at that authority now.

Three

Our Calling and Anointing in Christ

To understand our calling and authority in the area of deliverance, let's begin with Jesus' mission statement, which He read aloud in the synagogue in Nazareth at the start of His ministry:

> "The Spirit of the Lord GOD is upon Me, because the LORD has anointed Me to preach good tidings to the poor; He has sent Me to heal the brokenhearted, to proclaim liberty to the captives, and the opening of the prison to those who are bound; to proclaim the acceptable year of the LORD, and the day of vengeance of our God; to comfort all who mourn, to console those who mourn in Zion, to give them beauty for ashes, the oil of joy for mourning, the garment of praise for the spirit of heaviness; that they may be called trees of righteousness, the planting of the LORD, that He may be glorified."
>
> Isaiah 61:1–3

Jesus was sent by His Father to heal the brokenhearted. He came to set the prisoners free and to proclaim liberty to the captives. We saw in the first chapter how beaten up, downtrodden and brokenhearted the world is. So many people in our churches are in bondage to things like anger, fear, lust and perversion (just to name a few), with tangible symptoms like nightmares, eating disorders and depression. Jesus was sent to destroy the works of the devil, and He has assigned us this task until He returns.

After Jesus read Isaiah 61, He concluded by saying, "Today this Scripture is fulfilled in your hearing" (Luke 4:21). Not only was His statement given for that day and hour, but I believe it was a prophetic statement for us—for today! Jesus is the same yesterday, today and forever. He has commissioned us to go and make disciples of all nations, teaching them the things He has taught us.

Jesus left Nazareth and traveled to Capernaum to teach in the synagogue, and we are told that a man there "had a spirit of an unclean demon" (Luke 4:33). The man began shouting, and Jesus cast the evil spirit out. Now I cannot show you this in Scripture, but I have a strong feeling that this man was a member of that synagogue. He probably sat in the same seat week after week. Jesus' anointing provoked that spirit and the man was delivered from his bondage—just as we saw in the last chapter concerning the woman in Mexico.

I have seen this same thing happen many times in many places. The anointing of the Holy Spirit causes demons to manifest, because where the Spirit of the Lord is, there is freedom. His anointing breaks every yoke of bondage.

Not only have we been commissioned to carry out the ministry of deliverance, but we have also been given the authority and power to do so. It is through the name of Jesus that we gain this authority. Mark 16:17 quotes Jesus as saying: "And these signs will follow those who believe: In My name they will cast out demons." The apostle Paul wrote these words: "Therefore God exalted him to the highest place and gave him the name that is above every name, that at the name of Jesus every knee should bow, in heaven and on earth and under the earth, and every tongue confess that Jesus Christ is Lord, to the glory of God the Father" (Philippians 2:9–11, NIV).

Jesus actually gave us the right and privilege to use His name, the name that is above every name. We are ambassadors for Christ. We are His representatives here on this earth. We must exercise the authority and the power that come through His name.

The Spoken Word

It is interesting to note that even Jesus' physical presence did not necessarily change circumstances—generally people were not delivered or healed until He spoke. When Jesus went to the tomb of Lazarus, for instance, as recorded in John 11, nothing happened until He called out to Lazarus. When Jesus told Lazarus to come forth, he did so. I have heard it taught that if Jesus had not been specific in saying, "Lazarus, come forth!" every dead person in the tomb would have come out.

Matthew 8:23–27 also demonstrates the power of Jesus' spoken word:

Now when He got into a boat, His disciples followed Him. And suddenly a great tempest arose on the sea, so that the boat was covered with the waves. But He was asleep. Then His disciples came to Him and awoke Him, saying, "Lord, save us! We are perishing!"

But He said to them, "Why are you fearful, O you of little faith?" Then He arose and rebuked the winds and the sea, and there was a great calm. So the men marveled, saying, "Who can this be, that even the winds and the sea obey Him?"

Jesus was in the boat when the storm hit. Jesus' presence did not prevent the storm from coming or stop its rage. Nothing happened until Jesus spoke. But when He rebuked the wind and the sea, there came "a great calm."

In the next scene of that story, we see that Jesus crossed the lake to the region of the Gerasenes and was met by a man who was obviously demon-possessed. Jesus' presence certainly provoked the demons, but they did not leave until Jesus said, "Go."

If you study this Scripture, you will see how Jesus engaged these demons in a rather lengthy conversation. It even appears that Jesus may have experienced some degree of difficulty in casting out the legion of demons in this demoniac. History tells us the Pharisees followed a formula, or ritual, for exorcism.[1] The formula required the exorcist first to ask the name of the demon. Knowing the name apparently gave the exorcist authority or power over the demon and aided in driving it out. It almost seems as if Jesus reverted to this Pharisaic formula in dealing with Legion.

Jesus came to destroy the works of the devil and to advance the Kingdom of God; He did it with words and we can, in His name, do the same: "Behold, I give you the authority to trample on serpents and scorpions, and over all the power of the enemy, and nothing shall by any means hurt you" (Luke 10:19). Furthermore, we read in John 14:12 that Jesus declared: "Most assuredly, I say to you, he who believes in Me, the works that I do he will do also; and greater works than these he will do."

I would be happy just doing the works that Jesus did, wouldn't you? But He has promised us greater works.

> When the sun was setting, all those who had any that were sick with various diseases brought them to Him; and He laid His hands on every one of them and healed them. And demons also came out of many, crying out and saying, "You are the Christ, the Son of God!"

And He, rebuking them, did not allow them to speak,
for they knew that He was the Christ.

Luke 4:40–41

When evening had come, they brought to Him many who
were demon-possessed. And He cast out the spirits with a
word, and healed all who were sick.

Matthew 8:16

Imagine doing greater works than these! I am looking forward to the day when we can cast out demons with only a
word, and we can heal all who are sick. It is possible!

The Full Anointing

A young man on one of my deliverance teams came to me
one day with a legitimate question: "If Jesus cast demons
out with but a word, why does it sometimes take us hours
or even days to cast them out?"

I said to him, "We do not have the same anointing Jesus
had."

The Holy Spirit spoke to me immediately and said, *That
is not correct. There is only one anointing and you do have it.
You just are not yet walking in the fullness of it.*

Now you may think you do not have any anointing on
your life, but you do. You may not feel it or know it, but it
is there. First John 2:20 reminds us: "You have an anointing
from the Holy One" (NIV). This is shown to us by the Holy
Spirit each and every day.

Look at this anointing in Jesus' earliest followers:

Then the seventy returned with joy, saying, "Lord, even the
demons are subject to us in Your name."

Luke 10:17

[People] brought the sick out into the streets and laid them on beds and couches, that at least the shadow of Peter passing by might fall on some of them. Also a multitude gathered from the surrounding cities to Jerusalem, bringing sick people and those who were tormented by unclean spirits, and they were all healed.

Acts 5:15–16

Then Philip went down to the city of Samaria and preached Christ to them. And the multitudes with one accord heeded the things spoken by Philip, hearing and seeing the miracles which he did. For unclean spirits, crying with a loud voice, came out of many who were possessed; and many who were paralyzed and lame were healed.

Acts 8:5–8

Now it happened, as we went to prayer, that a certain slave girl possessed with a spirit of divination met us, who brought her masters much profit by fortune-telling. This girl followed Paul and us, and cried out, saying, "These men are the servants of the Most High God, who proclaim to us the way of salvation." And this she did for many days.

But Paul, greatly annoyed, turned and said to the spirit, "I command you in the name of Jesus Christ to come out of her." And he came out that very hour.

Acts 16:16–18

Now God worked unusual miracles by the hands of Paul, so that even handkerchiefs or aprons were brought from his body to the sick, and the diseases left them and the evil spirits went out of them.

Acts 19:11–12

Do you see the anointing? Do you see the power of God? I want you to know that the saving power of God did not die with the apostles, nor did the healing power of God, nor did the delivering power of God. Church history shows this to be true. The early Church was extremely active in the ministry of deliverance. Matthew Henry's commentary on Mark 16:17 gives us this insight:

> They shall cast out devils; this power was more common among Christians than any other, and lasted longer [than the apostles' lifetimes], as appears by the testimonies of Justin Martyr, Origen, Irenaeus, Tertullian, Minutius Felix, and others, cited by Grotius on this place.[2]

The Catholic Encyclopedia, in the section entitled "Exorcist," gives these facts: The practice of exorcism was not confined to only clerics, according to church father Origen, who states, "Even the simplest and rudest of the faithful sometimes cast out demons, by a mere prayer."[3] Martin of Tours was also said to be in the habit of casting out demons by prayer alone, without the laying on of hands.[4] Pope Cornelius wrote a letter from Rome sometime around AD 251–252 in which he spoke of 52 exorcists in Rome at that time.[5] One of the duties of an exorcist was "baptismal exorcism" in which "catechumens [people who were candidates for baptism] were exorcised [prayed for in a deliverance session] every day, for some time before baptism."[6]

According to the *History of the Christian Church*, by about the middle of the third century the exorcist was a recognized office of the Church. The exorcist was one "who by praying and the laying on of hands, cast out evil spirits from the possessed and the catechumens, and frequently assisted in baptism."[7]

New Dictionary of Theology explains that the early Church took the connection between baptism and deliverance very seriously. By the fourth century, exorcism was a common element in the baptismal rite.[8]

Regaining Our Roots

It is easy to see that the Church has strayed from her roots and her early teachings in the area of deliverance. By doing so, the Church has, in fact, moved away from the truth and power of God. The following is an excerpt from *Barnes' Notes on the New Testament*. This is a classic example of the error that has befallen the Church of Jesus Christ.

> And these signs shall follow them that believe; In my name shall they cast out devils; they shall speak with new tongues. . . .
>
> Mark 16:17 KJV

> *And these signs*: these miracles. These evidences that they are sent from God. *Them that believe*: the apostles, and those in the primitive age who were endowed with like power. This promise was fulfilled, if it can be shown that these signs followed in the case of any who believed, and it is not necessary to suppose that they would follow in the case of all. The meaning is that they would be the result of faith, or of the belief of the Gospel. It is true that they were. These signs were shown in the case of the apostles and early Christians. The infidel cannot say that the promise has not been fulfilled unless he can show that this never occurred; the Christian should be satisfied that the promise was fulfilled, if these miracles were ever actually wrought, though they do not occur now; and the believer now should not expect a miracle in his case. Miracles were necessary for the establishment of religion in the world; they are not necessary for its continuance now.[9]

These teachings, combined with extremes and abuses, have no doubt had a major part in thwarting God's plans for deliverance and healing and other miracles. It follows that teachings like these could be delaying the Church from fulfilling God's plan for her, and, ultimately, delaying the return of Jesus Christ for His Bride. It is time that we stop just speaking about these truths. We need to start living them and ministering in them. These truths are like the very bread on our tables. Consider, in fact, how Jesus refers to the ministry of deliverance in the account of the Syro-Phoenician woman who seeks His help for her little daughter:

> From there He arose and went to the region of Tyre and Sidon. And He entered a house and wanted no one to know it, but He could not be hidden. For a woman whose young daughter had an unclean spirit heard about Him, and she came and fell at His feet. The woman was a Greek, a Syro-Phoenician by birth, and she kept asking Him to cast the demon out of her daughter. But Jesus said to her, "Let the children be filled first, for it is not good to take *the children's bread* and throw it to the little dogs."
>
> And she answered and said to Him, "Yes, Lord, yet even the little dogs under the table eat from the children's crumbs."
>
> Then He said to her, "For this saying go your way; the demon has gone out of your daughter."
>
> And when she had come to her house, she found the demon gone out, and her daughter lying on the bed.
>
> Mark 7:24–30, emphasis added

We are the children and deliverance is our bread! The same cannot be said for unbelievers because they would not be able to "walk out" their deliverance—the doors that let in the demonic oppression would remain open. According to Matthew 12:43–45, the final condition of that person who has swept his house clean would be worse than the first.

As believers we have a calling, and we are given the authority to fulfill that calling. As we move in the anointing that the Lord has given us, we can and will conquer the authority and power of the enemy. Ephesians 1:22 says,

"[God the Father] put all things under [Jesus'] feet, and gave Him to be head over all things to the church." Ephesians 2:6 states, "[He has] raised us up together, and made us sit together in the heavenly places in Christ Jesus." If we are sitting with Christ and all things are under His feet, then they are under our feet as well!

FOUR

Reality of the Spirit Realm

When I first got saved, I had no comprehension of the spirit realm. I had been a drunk and drug addict all of my adult life. When people talked about ghosts, haunted houses, demons or witches, I would say to them, "You are *&%*# nuts! There are no such things." I was clueless. My concept of the spirit realm was *Casper and Friends*. Even after I got saved, I did not think much about it. I read the gospel accounts of Jesus' dealings with demons, but still this area had no reality.

My first experience with the demonic was at the Brownsville Revival early in 1997. It was about one in the morning and the crowds were leaving. I was sitting on the platform with two other students from the Bible school. We had been "catchers" that evening, standing behind those receiving prayer in the event they fell to the floor under the power of God.

All of a sudden, someone came into the church, yelling for help. The woman who was in charge of the prayer team headed for the front door, so the three of us followed her to offer our assistance. When we got outside, the scene was chaotic. At first it looked as if a crowd of people was beating up a young girl. At the instruction of the prayer team leader we moved into the crowd, picked up the girl, carried her into the sanctuary and placed her on the floor. All the while she was cursing in a voice obviously not her own and displaying superhuman, supernatural strength. The three of us were being raised up off the floor, literally, by a 98-pound teenager who was obviously demon-possessed. A member of the Brownsville deliverance team finally bound those spirits, much to our relief.

Afterward a member of the prayer team asked me if I was all right. I replied, "I don't think so!" It was the most bizarre thing I had ever experienced. I was visibly shaken. The leaders prayed peace over me and sent me home.

When I got into my vehicle, I said, "Lord, what in the world was that?"

The Lord spoke to me in what seemed to be an audible voice. He said, *I could not have shown you this in a classroom. I have placed you on a fast track; you are going to see a lot more in the area of deliverance.* I did begin to see more, and it has never stopped.

For many years in recent history the Church sidelined the topic of demons, assuming that demons operated only in Third World countries like Mexico or India. Missionaries were the only ones who talked about demons, so everyone assumed all the demons were on foreign soil. Seeing little relevance for their congregations, pastors did not teach or preach about demons.

In case you have any question, I want you to know that demons are just as real in downtown America as they are anywhere else in the world.

In primitive cultures, people worship objects around them: a large rock, a large tree, a totem (ashtoreth) pole or some other thing in nature. The things they worship are inanimate; they have no power or authority. But whenever a demon power or principality or some other host of wickedness is given squatter's rights, it takes authority over the people that desire to worship it. It starts feeding off their praise and idolatry, as well as their sacrifices, and it gains power.

Even though we do not make sacrifices to rocks or trees or poles, any time we give place to sin, we give place to a wicked spirit. When we walk in disobedience, we feed that demon. And in doing so, we are no different from people who put bowls of rice in front of a statue in some faraway land. Satan and his demons have no power, except for what we give them. When Adam sinned, he gave Satan his dominion and authority over the earth, but 2,000 years ago Jesus Christ reclaimed that power and authority.

Scriptural Precedent

Winkie Pratney has been quoted as saying, "The spirit realm is more real than this wall. Jesus proved that to us by walking through a wall twice after His resurrection."

> Then, the same day at evening, being the first day of the week, when the doors were shut where the disciples were assembled, for fear of the Jews, Jesus came and stood in the midst, and said to them, "Peace be with you."
>
> John 20:19

> And after eight days His disciples were again inside, and Thomas with them. Jesus came, the doors being shut, and stood in the midst, and said, "Peace to you!" Then He said to Thomas, "Reach your finger here, and look at My hands; and reach your hand here, and put it into My side. Do not be unbelieving, but believing."
>
> John 20:26–27

In this second instance, Jesus wanted to deal with Thomas' unbelief, but He also wanted to help us understand the reality of the spirit realm. I believe any time Scripture states the same thing more than once, God is emphasizing a point.

Years ago I jotted down an explanation that Neil Anderson gave as a basis for understanding the reality and work of demons:

> How do you think Satan carries on his worldwide ministry of evil and deception? He is a created being. He is not omnipresent, omniscient, or omnipotent. He cannot be everywhere in the world tempting and deceiving millions of people at the same moment. He does so through an army of emissaries (demons, evil spirits, fallen angels, etc.) who propagate his plan of rebellion around the world. It is clear from the context of Ephesians 6:12 that the rulers, powers, and forces which oppose us are spiritual entities in the heavenlies, in the spirit realm, in the spiritual world.[1]

Some people believe demons are fallen angels, while others believe they are spirits from a pre-Adamic race of people. The truth is, we do not know where they came from. We know only that they are disembodied spirit beings of unknown origin. I tend to believe that they are a portion of the one-third of the angels who fell with Satan. This is encouraging if you think about it. That means two-thirds of the angels are still on the job, on our side, and I like two-to-one odds.

I do want you to note that, as Neil Anderson has pointed out, the Bible does not attempt to prove the existence of demons; it simply records their activity. We can, however, glean much from the examples in Scripture, as you will see in the list below. From two verses in Luke alone we can draw the first seven points:

> "When an unclean spirit goes out of a man, he goes through dry places, seeking rest; and finding none, he says, 'I will

return to my house from which I came.' And when he comes, he finds it swept and put in order. Then he goes and takes with him seven other spirits more wicked than himself, and they enter and dwell there; and the last state of that man is worse than the first."

Luke 11:24–26

From this and various other Scriptures we discover:

1. Demons are invisible spirit beings that do not have physical bodies. They can exist inside or outside of humans, and they consider human bodies their homes. We also know from Matthew 8:31–32 that they can and will go into animals as a second choice: "So the demons begged Him, saying, 'If You cast us out, permit us to go away into the herd of swine.' And He said to them, 'Go.' So when they had come out, they went into the herd of swine."
2. They are able to travel at will.
3. They are able to communicate with each other. (Note: Numerous Scriptures show us they can and do communicate with humans as well.)
4. They are intelligent beings, able to remember and evaluate situations. They are also able to make plans and decisions.
5. They all have separate identities, yet are able to combine forces.
6. They have varying degrees of wickedness. Ephesians 6:12 also tells us they have varying degrees of rank in Satan's kingdom: "For we do not wrestle against flesh and blood, but against principalities, against powers, against the rulers of the darkness of this age, against spiritual hosts of wickedness in the heavenly places."
7. They torment and harm in varying degrees.

8. They can speak through a person they indwell. Language is not a barrier.
9. They can cause physical sickness and disease, such as deafness, blindness, crippling, bleeding.
10. They can cause depression and other mental disorders, including suicide.
11. They often manifest physically by throwing down the person they inhabit, causing convulsions and foaming at the mouth.
12. They often manifest with superhuman strength.
13. Demons can drive people to do things they would not ordinarily do, such as adultery, murder, perversion and the like.

The list goes on and on! The more I learn about the spirit realm, the more I realize how little we really know about it.

The Enemy Revealed

Jesus wants us to see the reality of the spirit realm, but there is another aspect that He wants us to see. Look at the account of Lucifer's fall given by the prophet Isaiah:

"How you are fallen from heaven, O Lucifer, son of the morning! How you are cut down to the ground, you who weakened the nations! For you have said in your heart: 'I will ascend into heaven, I will exalt my throne above the stars of God; I will also sit on the mount of the congregation on the farthest sides of the north; I will ascend above the heights of the clouds, I will be like the Most High.' Yet you shall be brought down to Sheol, to the lowest depths of the Pit. *Those who see you will gaze at you, and consider you, saying: 'Is this the man who made the earth tremble, who shook kingdoms, who made the world as a wilderness and destroyed its cities?'*"

Isaiah 14:12–17, emphasis added

This is a familiar passage of Scripture. It contains the "I wills" that got Lucifer in hot water to begin with. But note what verses 16–17 tell us: One day we are going to see Satan for what he is, and we are going to be absolutely amazed at what we see! We are going to say, "Is this the one? This is the punk that I let steal my peace, my joy, my marriage, my children, my finances? I cannot believe I let him cause all that hell in my life." We will be amazed on that day!

Jesus wants us to know the spirit realm is real, and He wants us to understand it fully. In part 2 we will unmask a number of the actions that open us up to spiritual consequences. These points of entry or open doors can all be closed. In part 3 we will learn how that is done.

Part 2

Points of Entry

Five

Sin: The Number One Open Door

At a Cleansing Stream retreat several years ago a young woman was manifesting on the prayer line. I went to assist the person praying with her and learned that it was a witchcraft spirit that was wrenching her so violently, and it refused to leave. I tried to calm this young woman and find out if she had a background in witchcraft. She assured me she had been a Christian all her life and had never experienced anything like this before. She had never even read a horoscope. But I could not free her from the demonic spirit. I then tried dealing with a generational spirit of witchcraft, also with no success.

We finally prayed for the Holy Spirit to show us what was going on with her. Almost immediately, she asked, "Could it be my job as a funeral director?"

"Yes," I told her, "exposure to the dead could explain this. But a legal right has somehow been given to the spirit."

We proceeded to pray for the Holy Spirit to show her what right this spirit had obtained. At that point she remembered her very first day on the job. It was also her first encounter with a dead body. The funeral director who was training her pulled the sheet off the body of a person he was going to embalm. He then asked her if the procedure bothered her. She responded with a "little white lie." "No," she said. "It does not bother me."

At that point the door was opened. The witchcraft spirit that was hanging onto that dead body went through the open door. She repented for the lie and renounced the spirit of witchcraft. It left immediately.

I tell you this story to illustrate the fact that there is no such thing as a small sin. All sin has consequences and can be a point of entry for the enemy. One false comment—one lie, one act of sin—by this young woman had opened the way for demonic oppression.

Sin is the number one entry point for demonic bondage. When we sin, we open a door in the spirit realm. Whatever demon is passing by or hanging around when that door is opened simply steps in. Sin has given it the legal right to stay.

Feeding Sin

Every time we sin, we feed whatever spirit is oppressing us. In Mexico I watched as people put bowls of rice or beans in front of idols in order to feed them. When we sin, we do the same thing. When we lie, we feed that lying spirit. When we look at pornography, we feed that perverse spirit. Each time we feed a spirit, it gets stronger.

When I first got saved, a pastor shared a story with me about an old Indian who raised dogs. He would train them to fight against each other and then he took bets on which one would win. One day a man noticed the

Indian always won. He always knew which dog would win. Finally the man cornered the old Indian and asked him how he knew which dog would win. The old Indian said, "It's easy. The dog I feed always wins. He has the strength to win."

It is no different with us. If we feed on spiritual junk—most television shows and movies fit this profile—we will lose. But if we feed our spirits with the things of God, the Word of God, praise, worship and prayer we will have the strength needed to win the battle.

I often tell the story I read once of an ingenious father's illustration of sin.[1] His teenage children were begging to see a movie rated PG–13. They gave him all the reasons that the movie would be entertaining—even harmless. All the kids were seeing it. Many people from their church found it entertaining. It had their favorite actors and a great script. It just had the suggestion of sex—nothing really happened. And the language was not too bad. And on and on. But the father refused steadfastly to let them go.

Later that evening this father asked his teens if they would like some brownies he had prepared. He told them that he had taken the family's favorite recipe and added something new. When they asked what the new thing was, he replied that he had added a special ingredient—dog poop.

He said that there was only a little bit of dog poop in the brownies. All the other ingredients were gourmet quality. He had taken great care to bake the brownies at the precise temperature for the exact time. He was sure the brownies would be superb. They would hardly notice the difference.

When the teens refused even a small taste, he explained that the movie they wanted to see was just like the brownies. Sin enters our minds and our homes by deceiving us into believing that just a "little bit" of evil will not matter. With the brownies, just a little bit made all the difference between a great brownie and a totally unacceptable product. He explained that not everything the world around us approves of is really acceptable.

Think of this the next time the devil comes to you and whispers, "It's just a little thing" or "Everyone is doing it" or "It's just a little sin. It's not that bad!"

It is that bad. When we sin, we violate a law. A line has been crossed and a transgression has occurred. Scripture shows that the regulations intended to be blessings for us become curses when we violate them. Ignorance is no excuse: Sin must be repented of. Sin is rebellion, which is the same as witchcraft (see 1 Samuel 15:23). Some people opened themselves to rebellion as children and continue to deal with it all of their adult lives. All sin opens doors for the enemy to torment us.

Facing Consequences

I have heard Pastor Jack Hayford give this illustration. Suppose, for example, a sign says, New Grass. Keep Off. We decide to walk through the restricted area anyway, only to find ourselves sinking. The sign failed to say the sod is quite wet. Now our shoes are covered with mud. It looked harmless to disobey the sign, but this has made a mess. If not cleaned off, the mud will eventually dry and leave a residue. If there was fertilizer in the newly sown grass, the chemicals might ruin our shoes. The chemicals may even cause infection if they come in contact with a cut or open blister.

This is a parallel, or picture, of what happens in the spirit realm when we sin. What appears to be a minor thing, like taking a short cut through that new grass, turns into a major disaster. All we have done is make a mess for ourselves. Now we have to deal with the consequences of our decision. We have to deal with the residue of sin.

I believe that the consequences of sin are often evident or manifest in sickness. I believe that all sickness and disease is of the devil, and sin opens the door. Now in saying that sickness is a manifestation of sin, I am not saying that someone who is sick is in sin or has a demon. We do, however, live in a fallen, dying world, and sickness is a precursor to death! Bad choices such as overeating, smoking, drinking alcohol and using illegal drugs can also give the devil a legal right to torment us with sickness and disease.

Remember what God told Adam would happen if he ate from the forbidden tree: "You shall surely die." After their sin of rebellion, neither Adam nor Eve died immediately in the physical sense, but they started dying the very moment they ate the forbidden fruit. I believe that sickness entered the world at that point.

Sexual Sins

While sin is the number one entry point for demonic bondage, sexual misconduct—in all its forms of immorality and perversion—is the most prevalent area of sin that allows demonic entry into our lives.

It is no coincidence that in several lists of sins in the Bible, sexual misconduct is at the top:

> Do you not know that the unrighteous will not inherit the kingdom of God? Do not be deceived. Neither fornicators, nor idolaters, nor adulterers, nor homosexuals, nor sodomites, nor thieves, nor covetous, nor drunkards, nor revilers, nor extortioners will inherit the kingdom of God. And such were some of you. But you were washed, but you were sanctified, but you were justified in the name of the Lord Jesus and by the Spirit of our God.
>
> 1 Corinthians 6:9–11

> Now the works of the flesh are evident, which are: adultery, fornication, uncleanness, lewdness, idolatry, sorcery, hatred, contentions, jealousies, outbursts of wrath, selfish ambi-

tions, dissensions, heresies, envy, murders, drunkenness, revelries, and the like; of which I tell you beforehand, just as I also told you in time past, that those who practice such things will not inherit the kingdom of God.

Galatians 5:19–21

Notice that Paul was not writing to people in the bars of Corinth and Galatia. No, he was writing to people in the churches of Corinth and Galatia!

Regarding sexual misconduct, I would add that although masturbation is not named specifically in these lists, it is, along with adultery and fornication, a "work of the flesh" that invites all the consequences of sin. Some people believe masturbation is a gift that God has given us for self-gratification. Let's set the record straight. When people masturbate they fantasize, and they do not fantasize about a new Buick. Jesus said, "If you look upon a woman with lust, you have already committed adultery" (see Matthew 5:28). Leviticus 15:16–17 says: "If any man has an emission of semen, then he shall wash all his body in water, and be unclean until evening. And any garment and any leather on which there is semen, it shall be washed with water, and be unclean until evening."

Why is sexual sin particularly insidious? Because anyone who engages in sexual activity with someone other than his or her spouse—and this includes masturbation—creates a soul tie with that person, which needs to be broken. This is true even if the other person is just an image from a magazine or the Internet.

This term *soul tie* is not found in Scripture, but the concept is, particularly in the use of the words *knit* and *cleave*. *Knit* means to be linked or tied or bound together, to cause to grow together. *Cleave* means to adhere to, fasten together, to be glued to or joined to. Soul ties, then, mean simply that our souls—our minds, wills and emotions—attach to everyone we become intimate with. We can have godly and ungodly soul ties to persons, places and things.

A godly soul tie is the kind of bond formed between a man and woman as a married couple. Jesus said: "For this reason a man shall leave his father and mother and be joined to his wife, and the two shall become *one flesh*" (Matthew 19:5, emphasis added).

Another example of a godly soul tie is one that is not sexual but emotional. This example is found in 1 Samuel 18:1: "The soul of Jonathan was knit to the soul of David, and Jonathan loved him *as his own soul*" (emphasis added).

This kind of connection is a good and healthy union, the joining of man and woman in marriage or the bonding of close friends. In the case of sinful relations, however, particularly when the relations are sexual, ungodly soul ties are formed. Paul gives this explanation:

> Or do you not know that he who is joined to a harlot is one body with her? For "the two," He says, "shall become one flesh." . . .
> Flee sexual immorality. Every sin that a man does is outside the body, but he who commits sexual immorality sins against his own body.
>
> 1 Corinthians 6:16, 18

Genesis 34:1–3 illustrates how an ungodly soul tie can be formed from illicit unions:

> Now Dinah the daughter of Leah, whom she had borne to Jacob, went out to see the daughters of the land. And when Shechem the son of Hamor the Hivite, prince of the country, saw her, he took her and lay with her, and violated her. His soul was strongly attracted to Dinah.

Shechem raped the young woman, and an ungodly soul tie was created between them. The King James Version says, "His soul clave unto Dinah." He was *glued* to Dinah.

In other words, regardless of the circumstances surrounding the sexual union, the two truly do become one. Whenever these people separate and for whatever reason they separate, there is a tearing away of their souls. Think of it like this. If I take two pieces of paper and glue them together, then try to tear them apart, each page will be missing large pieces and will have part of the other page still glued to it.

Many people, including people in our churches, are missing pieces of their souls and are walking around, looking to fill the void created by ungodly sexual encounters. Other people are carrying junk around from former sexual partners and are struggling with baggage that does not even belong to them. In the 1970s it seemed that everywhere you turned someone was "trying to find" himself or herself. I wonder how many of those people were suffering the effects of the free love (that is, free sex) movement of the 1960s. It is important to note that persons who had sexual encounters prior to their marriages entered marriage with an unholy union. They should repent and make their marriages holy.

In deliverance ministry we deal with many people who are suffering from the effects of soul ties. When the two became one, one person's garbage became the other person's garbage. Quite often a spirit of perversion comes in as a result of these ungodly soul ties. This can and does lead to other perversions such as homosexuality, bisexuality, bestiality, molestation and incest. When we engage in perversion, our souls become open to guilt, shame and condemnation, especially after we get saved! The devil loves nothing more than to bombard our minds with the sins of our pasts.

Sin, whether lying, immoral sex, murder or stealing, creates a point of entry in our lives for the enemy to exploit and establish strongholds. I believe that it is the number one weapon the enemy uses against us. We need to be on guard against his schemes and stand firm in the truth of God's Word so that we can stand blameless before God and help others become so free.

Six

Curses: Five Sources

The next point of entry through which the enemy gains ground in our lives is curses. There are five areas of curses that affect us to varying degrees:

1. Word curses spoken over us by ourselves or others.
2. Curses that result from the consequences of our own personal sins.
3. Curses inherited from our forefathers and foremothers due to their sins.
4. Curses brought on as a judgment due to a broken vow to God.
5. Curses placed on us by those who practice witchcraft and sorcery.

1. Spoken Words

Most people probably think of a word curse as a deliberate infliction of harm. Oftentimes, however, we do not realize that words spoken to us and words we speak in normal conversation have enormous destructive power. Look, for example, at the repercussions from these words spoken by the children of Israel:

> They traveled from Mount Hor along the route to the Red Sea, to go around Edom. But the people grew impatient on the way; they spoke against God and against Moses, and said, *"Why have you brought us up out of Egypt to die in the desert? There is no bread! There is no water! And we detest this miserable food!"*
>
> Numbers 21:4–5, NIV, emphasis added

History attests to the power of their complaining and criticizing words. All but two of the estimated millions of Israelites who left Egypt died in the wilderness. We need to understand the power of the spoken word for good or ill, for, as we will see in a moment, no word is without effect. No word is lost.

God's Decree

The power of words can be traced back to the beginning. God Himself initiated this sequence:

> In the beginning God created the heavens and the earth. The earth was without form, and void; and darkness was on the face of the deep. And the Spirit of God was hovering over the face of the waters.
> *Then God said,* "Let there be light"; and there was light.
>
> Genesis 1:1–3, emphasis added

This verbal activity of God continued throughout Creation: "God called" (verse 5); "God said" (verse 6); "God called" (verse 8); "God said" (verse 9); "God called" (verse 10); "God said" (verse 11); "God said" (verse 14); "God said" (verse 20); "God blessed" (verse 22); "God said" (verse 24); "God said" (verse 26); "God blessed" (verse 28); and "God said" (verse 29).

God actually *decreed* the world into existence, and not just our world but all worlds: "By faith we understand that the worlds were framed by the word of God" (Hebrews 11:3). The whole universe, as endless as it is, was framed by the spoken Word of God.

But God did not stop there. The One who caused the universe to come into being has also given us the capacity to speak words that are creative. Genesis 1:26 says, "Then God said, 'Let Us make man in Our image.'" God's image is in us! Just like Him, we have a tremendous capacity of will. He has given us the power to make choices, right or wrong, good or bad, and He will *not* override our will. Many of us are not aware of, or do not understand, this truth. We make casual choices and offhand remarks without regard for the weight our words carry and the consequences they incur. When we speak, things happen in the spiritual realm. This, in turn, has an effect on the natural realm.

A decree is normally an executive order in a nation made by a president or king. You may recall the old movie *The Ten Commandments*. Whenever Pharaoh would decree, "So let it be written. So let it be done," you had better believe it was done just as he had declared it to be. Decrees are mandates that, when spoken, come to pass according to the power and the authority behind the one speaking them.

Well, as children of God and joint heirs with Christ we also make decrees when we speak—decrees that will stand! The Bible says that there is no sound made without significance: "There are, it may be, so many kinds of voices [languages] in the world, and none of them is without signification" (1 Corinthians 14:10, KJV). It is law in the spirit realm: Our words have power in them. When we speak, we make decrees. Proverbs 18:21 states: "Death and life are in the power of the tongue, and those who love it will eat its fruit."

Accountability

I once heard an amazing story about a World War II radio transmission. In the 1940s a Japanese radio transmission was sent to the Japanese military stationed in the Pacific. Apparently it was never received. Then one day in 1973 in Phoenix, Arizona, the regular programming of a rock and roll radio station was interrupted as this same Japanese military transmission was suddenly received by this station and played in its entirety. This broadcast had been traveling around the airways, lost for almost thirty years, yet still active. When the weather conditions were just right, it came forth.

Think about the personal implications: Every word you have ever spoken is traveling about the atmosphere. That is a scary thought, especially in light of Jesus' words in Matthew 12:36: "But I say to you that for every idle word men may speak, they will give account of it in the day of judgment."

Every word we speak has significance as well as consequences. Everyone of us will stand before God and give an account for every idle word. But praise God! We can bring those words under the blood of Jesus. Every reckless, careless, unwise, destructive and hateful word will be washed away when we repent and ask for forgiveness.

Jack Hayford teaches that the word *judgment*, as used in Matthew 12:36, signifies not only the specific day in which we will be accountable for our evil deeds but also the idea of deliverance. In other words, it signifies breaking a yoke. We need, therefore, to ask the Holy Spirit to bring to our minds the things we have said that we need to repent of—any unholy yoking that we need to break. We need to repent and ask God to blot those things out of His book: "For by your words you will be justified, and by your words you will be condemned" (Matthew 12:37).

Our words can get us into trouble, and they can get us out of trouble.

Righteous Use of the Tongue

We have seen that when God created the worlds with His words, He did three things: He *said*, He *called* and He *blessed*. What God *said*, came into being: "Then God said, 'Let there be light'; and there was light" (Genesis 1:3). He then *called* or named: "God called the light Day, and the darkness He called Night. So the evening and the morning were the first day" (Genesis 1:5).

In naming the light *day* and the darkness *night*, God gave them an identity. Later God gave Adam the assignment of naming all of the animals (see Genesis 2:19). Just as God had done with the rest of creation, Adam identified and named each creature. Whatever he called them was what they became.

I want you to know that many people you will minister to—in fact, many people you will simply come into contact with—are in bondage right now because of human words that identified them as things that they are not. They have been misnamed and misidentified by parents, teachers, friends, doctors, psychologists, psychiatrists or even themselves. A lot of us create our own problems by how we speak over ourselves. We do not even realize that we have become bound to our own words, accepting the conditions they create as "normal."

We may have heard—or said to ourselves—things like: "You're so stupid," "You're retarded," "You've got cancer," "You have mental illness," "You'll never amount to anything," "You're just like your father"—the list goes on and on! When something nice is said to us, we feel secure and affirmed. When something bad is said, we feel degraded and hurt. You or I may be capable of some achievement, but if someone tells us that we cannot do it, one of two things will happen. Either we will fall into self-doubt and not be able to do it, or we will grit our teeth and say, "I'll show him." In either case, the negative words worked against us.

Likewise when we yell at the bad driver swerving though traffic—"You idiot!"—we have no idea how our words will affect that individual. Words against him have been spoken into the atmosphere, and words that identify, that name something, have power. Certain words and attitudes we invoke are actually the names of spirits or demons. One such example is the spirit of divorce. Once you speak divorce in your household, you give it a license to hang out, to sow seed, to establish a stronghold. It is probably the most destructive word you can speak in your home. God wants us to identify things as they really are, not as we think they are!

After God *spoke* and *called*, He *blessed*. We need to start invoking the blessings of God and stop speaking curses. Ephesians 5:25–26 demonstrates a righteous use of the tongue in a relationship: "Husbands, love your wives, just as Christ also loved the church and gave Himself for her, that He might sanctify and cleanse her with the washing of water by the word." I have learned that words that nurture and nourish are words that bless. I bless my wife at every meal. I believe she gets prettier every day! The power of our words can be used in a positive way to bring blessings to those around us.

Look at how God blessed the work of His hands: "And God blessed them, saying, 'Be fruitful and multiply, and fill the waters in the seas, and let birds multiply on the earth'" (Genesis 1:22). Everything God blesses multiplies;

it multiplies life. When we speak blessings, we speak life into our lives and into the lives of others. A blessing is a joining of our hearts and our words. Romans 10:10 states: "For with the heart one believes unto righteousness, and with the mouth confession is made unto salvation."

With what? Made unto what? That which is believed in the heart is spoken forth with our mouths. "For out of the abundance of the heart the mouth speaks" (Matthew 12:34).

Reaping What We Sow

The principle of speech is a law, just like gravity. And as with any law, we have the opportunity to transgress or violate it. As we noted in our discussion of sin, the reason is not important. Whether we break a law through ignorance or rebellion, the outcome is the same: A violation of the law incurs a penalty. We reap what we sow.

When I went through deliverance soon after coming to Brownsville, the team working with me began calling up different spirits and strongholds. Throughout the prayers, I did a lot of yawning and burped a few times. Truthfully, I was surprised. With a background as messed up as mine I pretty much expected to flop like a fish or to do something more demonstrative than yawn.

Then they called up a spirit of epilepsy. All of a sudden I fell out of my chair and landed on the floor. As I hit the floor I said out loud, "Where did that come from?" Immediately I heard the Lord say to me, *Let Me show you.*

The Lord then played a video in my mind that took me back 23 years. I was nineteen years old. I had stayed out partying on a Friday night till almost three in the morning. I came home drunk, fell into bed and got up just three hours later, still drunk. I showered and drove about two hours around the Washington Beltway to the University of Maryland in order to take a real estate licensing exam. I got in line and waited.

Finally, when my turn came, the individual in charge asked my name, checked me off the list and asked for a picture ID. I reached for my wallet and realized I had forgotten it. I told him, "I am an epileptic. I am not allowed to drive."

The man's eyes grew wide. He quickly handed me two number 2 pencils and a copy of the exam, sat me in the front row and watched me nervously for two hours or so until I finished the test and left. I laughed all the way to a liquor store, where I bought a six-pack and drove home. I never thought about it again until 23 years later while sitting on the floor in that deliverance session.

God showed me that when I had claimed epilepsy, I had given the enemy a legal right to inflict me with that disease by the words of my own mouth. I had said, "I am an epileptic." And the devil had replied, "You are now!"

I never had any symptoms of that disease, but I truly believe the enemy knew that God had plans for my life, and the devil was just waiting for an opportune time to inflict me with it in order to cause the most damage that he could. The assignment against me was still there. I repented and it left.

The Enemy's Plan

We are made in God's image, and the devil hates everything that looks like God. The enemy's intent is to controvert God's Word: His passion is to steal, kill and destroy, and he will use any means he can to do so. I believe he especially enjoys inflicting pain and torment on us in response to words we have cursed ourselves with, or words spoken against us by our loved ones.

We need to remember this:

> For though we walk in the flesh, we do not war according to the flesh. For the weapons of our warfare are not carnal

but mighty in God for pulling down strongholds, casting down arguments [speculations, imaginations] and every high thing that exalts itself against the knowledge of God, bringing every thought into captivity to the obedience of Christ.

2 Corinthians 10:3–5

The word used for "arguments" in verse 5 is *logismos*. It is a Greek word from which we get words like *logistics*, meaning "the art of calculating." It gives the sense of the power of words to "build up a case against you."[1] This is how strongholds are built in our hearts, homes, businesses and circumstances. God gave us the power and ability to use the spoken word to make decrees. When a decree makes a case against us and we accept it, we have given evil spirits a license to occupy our hearts and minds. As this logistical scene plays out, Satan can stand before God and say, "I have a right." He just plays the tape. He is the accuser of the brethren, and he is good at it.

But thank God that He is the righteous Judge! As we have seen, if we confess our sin, we are choosing to say the same thing God says about sin: It is wrong. What we are actually saying is, "I gave the adversary a legal right in this area, God, but now I see I was wrong. God, I cannot undo what was done, but You can. I repent." Once we see what we have done and repent, confessing it with our mouths, God sweeps in and by His power removes the enemy's right to stay. The Holy Spirit drives the enemy out.

We have got to stop stumbling through life blindly, doing and saying whatever we want. We have got to stop complaining and criticizing. We have got to stop placing judgments on ourselves and others. The Bible says whatever measure we judge with, we will be judged (see Matthew 7:2).

We need to speak life and not death, blessings and not curses. Here is a prayer of repentance that will help bring cleansing from judgmental words spoken in the past:

Heavenly Father, I ask You to bring to my memory every word curse I have spoken over others and myself. Reveal to me every idle word I have spoken in order that I might confess it and repent. I pray that the precious blood of Jesus will wash each one of them away.

Lord, I humbly ask that You guard my heart and my mouth from this moment on. In Jesus' name I pray, amen.

2. Personal Sin

We discussed sin in chapter 5. I simply want to note here that the sins we commit can be entry points for curses. Here are several Scriptures that make this clear.

In Exodus 15:26 we read: "If you diligently heed the voice of the LORD your God and do what is right in His sight, give ear to His commandments and keep all His statutes, I will put none of the diseases on you which I have brought on the Egyptians. For I am the LORD who heals you."

Deuteronomy 28:15 tells us: "But it shall come to pass, if you do not obey the voice of the LORD your God, to observe carefully all His commandments and His statutes which I command you today, that all these curses will come upon you and overtake you."

Jeremiah also spoke of curses as a consequence of disobedience: "Thus says the LORD God of Israel: 'Cursed is the man who does not obey the words of this covenant'" (Jeremiah 11:3).

Paul warned the Ephesians: "'Be angry, and do not sin'; do not let the sun go down on your wrath, nor give place to the devil" (Ephesians 4:26–27).

We must abide by God's spiritual law, or curses will overtake us—and, as we will see in a moment, our children as well. We can repent of sin and God will forgive us, but we may still have to deal with various consequences.

3. Inherited Curses

All families have three basic types of traits or characteristics that are passed down from generation to generation:

1. *Physical traits* such as blond hair and blue eyes. A family might have a mother and daughter who look exactly alike or a son who is the spitting image of his father.
2. *Soulish traits* such as likes and dislikes, attitudes, mannerisms. Positive traits might include generosity or hospitality. Negative traits might include racism, bigotry, depression, divorce, alcoholism or drug addiction.
3. *Spiritual traits* such as religious affiliation. You may hear comments like: "My mom was a Catholic, my grandmother was a Catholic and I am a Catholic" or "We have always been Pentecostals. In fact, my great-great-grandfather was at Azusa Street."

Just as these general traits are handed down, so are the effects of curses. Sometimes we find ourselves cursed because of the actions of our forefathers and foremothers back to the third, fourth, even the tenth generation and beyond. In some cases it is an actual demonic spirit that is passed on. These family spirits, or familiar spirits, which we will discuss in more detail in chapter 7, can move from generation to generation. These evil spirits feed on behaviors such as perversion, lust, adultery, fornication, incest and molestation.

The idea that sin and its consequences passes down from generation to generation is found in God's instructions to His people in the book of Exodus regarding idols:

"You shall not bow down to them nor serve them. For I, the LORD your God, am a jealous God, visiting the iniquity of the fathers *upon the children to the third and fourth generations of those who hate Me,* but showing mercy to thousands, to those who love Me and keep My commandments."

Exodus 20:5–6, emphasis added

This promise (yes, this is a promise of God) is repeated a few chapters later:

And the Lord passed before him and proclaimed, "The Lord, the Lord God, merciful and gracious, longsuffering, and abounding in goodness and truth, keeping mercy for thousands, forgiving iniquity and transgression and sin, by no means clearing the guilty, visiting the iniquity of the fathers *upon the children and the children's children to the third and the fourth generation.*"

Exodus 34:6–7, emphasis added

Later this passage is referred to in Moses' address to the next generation. Here he states that the descendants of a child born out of wedlock are cursed to the tenth generation: "One of illegitimate birth shall not enter the assembly of the Lord; even to the tenth generation none of his descendants shall enter the assembly of the Lord" (Deuteronomy 23:2).

Most of us have not had the pleasure of knowing past generations of family members. We probably have no idea if they loved or hated God. I did not know my grandfather, but based on my past and my father's past, I can imagine what my grandparents were like. We can see from our own lives that our sins affect not only our children, but their children and their children's children as well.

Biblical Examples

The Bible gives some amazing examples of generational curses and the effects they had on future generations. Look at these instances:

1. Adam and Eve sinned and introduced sickness and death into their family. Their son Cain murdered his brother, Abel, out of envy.
2. Noah became drunk and lay uncovered in his tent. His son Ham looked on his father's nakedness but did not respect him by covering him. Ham also announced it, thus further dishonoring his father. When Noah awoke, he cursed one of Ham's sons, Canaan. As the result of that perversion an entire people—the Canaanites—were, and still are, under a curse.
3. Abraham moved ahead of God's word that he and Sarah would have a child. He fathered a son in the flesh, thus robbing the birthright from the firstborn son. In the next five generations, the youngest prospered instead of the oldest. We also read in Scripture how Abraham chose to lie to Abimelech; a spirit of lying and deception is evident in his family line in the generations that followed. Jacob deceived his father, Isaac, and took the blessing due to Esau as the oldest son. Jacob's sons, in turn, lied to him about the disappearance of Joseph. They faked his death by tearing up his coat and putting animal blood on it, when they had really sold their brother into slavery.
4. David, the man after God's own heart, fell into sexual sin with Bathsheba. After committing adultery, he then murdered her husband, Uriah, and married Bathsheba to try to hide his sin. As a result, we see a history of incest, rape, rebellion and womanizing in David's children.
5. One of the most pronounced biblical accounts of a curse is the one placed on Eli and his family because of his disobedience:

> "In that day I will perform against Eli all that I have spoken concerning his house, from beginning to end. For I have told him that I will judge his house forever

for the iniquity which he knows, because his sons
made themselves vile, and he did not restrain them.
And therefore I have sworn to the house of Eli that
the iniquity of Eli's house shall not be atoned for by
sacrifice or offering forever."

1 Samuel 3:12–14

I would sure hate to be in that family line, wouldn't
you? Let's look at the specifics of the curse:

Then a man of God came to Eli and said to him, "Thus
says the LORD: 'Did I not clearly reveal Myself to the
house of your father when they were in Egypt in
Pharaoh's house? Did I not choose him out of all the
tribes of Israel to be My priest, to offer upon My altar,
to burn incense, and to wear an ephod before Me?
And did I not give to the house of your father all the
offerings of the children of Israel made by fire? Why
do you kick at [scorn] My sacrifice and My offering
which I have commanded in My dwelling place, and
honor your sons more than Me, to make yourselves fat
with the best of all the offerings of Israel My people?'
Therefore the LORD God of Israel says: 'I said indeed
that your house and the house of your father would
walk [minister] before Me forever.' But now the LORD
says: 'Far be it from Me; for those who honor Me I
will honor, and those who despise Me shall be lightly
esteemed. Behold, the days are coming that I will cut
off your arm [cut short your strength] and the arm of
your father's house, *so that there will not be an old man
in your house* [family line]. *And you will see an enemy
in My dwelling place*, despite all the good which God
does for Israel. *And there shall not be an old man in your
house forever. But any of your men whom I do not cut off
from My altar shall consume your eyes* [blind your eyes
with tears] *and grieve your heart. And all the descendants
of your house shall die in the flower of their age.'"

1 Samuel 2:27–33, emphasis added

Wow! What a curse! Eli's disobedience brought grief to his family *forever*.

6. Curses are not limited to individuals and their descendants. The New Testament gives the account of the curse the nation of Israel spoke upon herself regarding Jesus' death:

> Pilate said to them, "What then shall I do with Jesus who is called Christ?"
> They all said to him, "Let Him be crucified!"
> Then the governor said, "Why, what evil has He done?"
> But they cried out all the more, saying, "Let Him be crucified!"
> When Pilate saw that he could not prevail at all, but rather that a tumult was rising, he took water and washed his hands before the multitude, saying, "I am innocent of the blood of this just Person. You see to it."
> And all the people answered and said, "His blood be on us and on our children."
>
> Matthew 27:22–25

These are just a few examples of the devastating effects of generational curses. But praise God! I want you to know there is good news to counter this generational effect. Jesus hung on a tree to take our curses upon Himself. Jesus paid the price. The torture, crucifixion and death of Jesus Christ provided complete atonement for every curse, every sickness and all sin.

Breaking Curses

Sometimes I think we do not realize the fullness of what His sacrifice means for us. Jesus bled from seven places. In Hebrew the number seven symbolizes completion. What did Jesus say before He died? He said, "It is finished!" (John 19:30).

A crown of thorns was forced onto His head, penetrating to His skull. Artistic renderings and theological interpretations alike suggest that these thorns circled the full circumference of His head.[2] This symbolizes to me the fact that Jesus paid the price for our mental health. His death atoned for our wholeness of mind. This means, therefore, that depression, mental illness, madness and insanity have no place and no right in a child of God.

His back was plowed open by a Roman scourge. By this shedding of blood, Jesus opened the way for us to receive physical healing: cancer, diabetes, blood disorders, blindness and lameness—no infirmity has a place in us for "by His stripes we are healed" (Isaiah 53:5). Jesus paid the price on Calvary.

Both of His hands and both of His feet were nailed to the cross, blood dripping from them. We prosper through the work of our hands. Our feet make us mobile and give us the ability to follow Him. The blood that dripped from His hands and feet gives us the power and strength to follow where He leads.

A Roman spear pierced Jesus' side, and water and blood gushed out of the wound. I believe that this demonstrates how His bleeding heart brings healing to our wounded hearts—our damaged emotions.

Acts 2:21 states this: "And it shall come to pass that whoever calls on the name of the LORD shall be saved." The Greek word used here for "save" comes from *sozo*. It is used in the New Testament to mean not only spiritual salvation, but also deliverance from danger, suffering and sickness.[3] Not only did the precious blood of Jesus pay for our sins so that we might be reconciled with His Father, but it also paid for our healing and our deliverance. "Christ has redeemed us from the curse of the law, having become a curse for us (for it is written, 'Cursed is everyone who hangs on a tree')" (Galatians 3:13).

This means that through the power of the blood of Jesus we can break any generational curse and be free from its effects. God's words to the Israelites demonstrate this principle:

> "'You will perish among the nations; the land of your enemies will devour you. Those of you who are left will waste away in the lands of their enemies because of their sins; also because of their fathers' sins they will waste away.
>
> *"'But if they will confess their sins and the sins of their fathers*—their treachery against me and their hostility toward me, which made me hostile toward them so that I sent them into the land of their enemies—then when their uncircumcised hearts are humbled and they pay for their sin, I will remember my covenant with Jacob and my covenant with Isaac and my covenant with Abraham, and I will remember the land. For the land will be deserted by them and will enjoy its sabbaths while it lies desolate without them. They will pay for their sins because they rejected my laws and abhorred my decrees. Yet in spite of this, when they are in the land of their enemies, I will not reject them or abhor them so as to destroy them completely, breaking my covenant with them. I am the LORD their God. *But for their sake I will remember the covenant with their ancestors whom I brought out of Egypt in the sight of the nations to be their God. I am the LORD.*'"
>
> Leviticus 26:38–45, NIV, emphasis added

Other verses affirm this:

> "O Lord, according to all Your righteousness, I pray, let Your anger and Your fury be turned away from Your city Jerusalem, Your holy mountain; because for our sins, and *for the iniquities of our fathers,* Jerusalem and Your people are a reproach to all those around us."
>
> Daniel 9:16, emphasis added

> "Then those of Israelite lineage separated themselves from all foreigners; and they stood and confessed their sins *and the iniquities of their fathers.*"
>
> Nehemiah 9:2, emphasis added

Are you getting the picture? We must repent not only for our sins but also for the sins of our ancestors.

After we confess our sins and the sins of our forefathers and foremothers, we then need to renounce the curses sin brought about and break them. If at all possible, it is best to break each curse specifically, by name. Here is an example of renouncing the curse of perversion:

> I repent of my sins and the sins of my forefathers and fore-mothers in the area of *perversion* back to the third, fourth, and even the tenth generation and beyond. I renounce and break every generational curse of *perversion* in my family on my mother's side and my father's side. I break it past, present and future, from this moment on, in Jesus' name, amen!

I will say it again: We reap what we sow. It is a spiritual law! Curses must be dealt with through the name of Jesus or they will continue through the generations.

4. Judgment for a Broken Vow

Broken vows are another point of entry through which Satan gains ground and establishes strongholds. The Scripture that follows illustrates the seriousness of a vow. Joshua and the Israelites were taking possession of the land given them by God, destroying the pagan cities in their path. The people of nearby Gibeon planned a ruse to save their lives.

> When the inhabitants of Gibeon heard what Joshua had done to Jericho and Ai, they worked craftily, and went and pretended to be ambassadors [coming from a faraway land]. And they took old sacks on their donkeys, old wineskins torn and mended. . . .
> So Joshua made peace with them, and made a covenant with them to let them live; and the rulers of the congregation swore to them.

And it happened at the end of three days, after they had made a covenant with them, that they heard that they were their neighbors who dwelt near them.

Joshua 9:3–4, 15–16

This oath was procured by trickery, but the elders of Israel declared to the congregation that it must be upheld:

"We have sworn to them by the LORD God of Israel; now therefore, we may not touch them. This we will do to them: We will let them live, lest wrath be upon us because of the oath which we swore to them."

Joshua 9:19–20

The story continues centuries later. During the reign of King David a severe famine had consumed the land for three years. The king sought an explanation from the Lord about the reason for their suffering:

And the LORD answered, "It is because of Saul and his bloodthirsty house, because he killed the Gibeonites." So the king called the Gibeonites and spoke to them. Now the Gibeonites were not of the children of Israel, but of the remnant of the Amorites; the children of Israel had sworn protection to them, but Saul had sought to kill them in his zeal for the children of Israel and Judah.

2 Samuel 21:1–2

King Saul had broken the vow that the people of Israel had made with the Gibeonites. As a result, Saul's descendants had to pay a price.

Therefore David said to the Gibeonites, "What shall I do for you? And with what shall I make atonement, that you may bless the inheritance of the LORD?"

And the Gibeonites said to him, "We will have no silver or gold from Saul or from his house, nor shall you kill any man in Israel for us."

So he said, "Whatever you say, I will do for you."

Then they answered the king, "As for the man who consumed us and plotted against us, that we should be destroyed from remaining in any of the territories of Israel, let seven men of his descendants be delivered to us, and we will hang them before the LORD in Gibeah of Saul, whom the LORD chose."

And the king said, "I will give them."

. . . And [after the men were hanged by the Gibeonites and their bones regathered by David] God heeded the prayer for the land.

2 Samuel 21:3–6, 14

A broken vow, a curse and a blood price paid.

Note also that the Bible warns against making a rash vow and outlines the consequences for doing so. As with any sin we commit, the pattern for freedom is always the same: We repent before God for sinning; we renounce the spirit empowered to enforce the curse; and we break its power from our lives.

5. The Effects of Witchcraft and Sorcery

Curses placed on us by those who practice witchcraft and sorcery can be powerful points of entry for the enemy to gain ground in our lives. These curses include all hexes, vexes, spells, chants, incantations, voodoo and the like. They are accomplished by conjuring up a demon and dispatching it to cause harm. Voodoo, for instance, is the practice of cursing an object that represents a person. A demon is then dispatched to afflict the person in the same way the object was cursed.

A lot of people (like myself before I was saved and became aware of the spirit realm) question the existence of witchcraft and all of the activity of witches, including curses. Scripture is full of instances of the activity of witchcraft, and warnings not to take part. Here is a prophetic word spoken about the fall of Babylon:

"Now then listen, you wanton creature, lounging in your security.... Loss of children and widowhood ... will come upon you in full measure, in spite of your many sorceries and all your potent spells. You have trusted in your wickedness and have said, 'No one sees me.' Your wisdom and knowledge mislead you when you say to yourself, 'I am, and there is none besides me.' Disaster will come upon you, and you will not know how to conjure it away. A calamity will fall upon you that you cannot ward off with a ransom; a catastrophe you cannot foresee will suddenly come upon you. Keep on, then, with your magic spells and with your many sorceries, which you have labored at since childhood. Perhaps you will succeed, perhaps you will cause terror. All the counsel you have received has only worn you out! Let your astrologers come forward, those stargazers who make predictions month by month, let them save you from what is coming upon you. Surely they are like stubble; the fire will burn them up. They cannot even save themselves from the power of the flame."

Isaiah 47:8–14, NIV

A lot of people argue that Christians cannot fall prey to a curse because of this verse: "Like a flitting sparrow, like a flying swallow, so a curse without cause shall not alight" (Proverbs 26:2). If a door has been opened for the enemy, however, and there is a cause, a curse can and will alight.

A few years ago I was attacked by a severe sickness. I prayed and prayed but the sickness persisted. I continued to cry out to God to show me why I was so sick. Finally God showed me in a dream a girl with whom our ministry team was working. In the dream she was dancing in a circle, doing something with her fingers. I knew that she was casting spells against me. When God showed me this girl cursing me, I quoted the above Scripture to the Lord in protest. His response to me was, *Check your attitude.* Apparently I had opened a door with a wrong attitude. I repented.

The next day I confronted the girl and asked her if she had been putting spells on people. She burst into tears and said she often did things with her hands that she did not want to do or mean to do. She would just find herself doing it.

She then told me that when she was twelve years old her parents had put her in a mental hospital where she was befriended by a witch. The witch had convinced her to cut her finger and draw an image on the floor using her own blood. After doing that, she heard something run across the room and jump into her chest. From that moment on, she had supernatural powers.

During this girl's deliverance session, her face contorted unnaturally and she attacked a team member. We later discovered that she had multiple personality disorder (MPD), which we will discuss in chapter 8. One of her personalities was an active sorceress.

In order to protect ourselves from witchcraft, we have to make sure that Satan has no legal right, no open doors through which to enter our lives.

There is one last thing I want to point out about curses in relation to witchcraft. Look at this warning in Scripture:

> "You shall burn the carved images of their gods with fire; you shall not covet the silver or gold that is on them, nor take it for yourselves, lest you be snared by it; for it is an abomination to the LORD your God. *Nor shall you bring an abomination into your house, lest you be doomed to destruction like it.* You shall utterly detest it and utterly abhor it, for it is an accursed thing."
>
> Deuteronomy 7:25–26, emphasis added

Masks, statues of Buddha and other idolatrous statues and objects will put a curse on anyone who brings them into his home. Janet and I received a call one day from a woman whose roommate was screaming, growling, cursing, crying, vomiting and being thrown violently around her room. We went to the apartment house immediately and worked with the woman in her room for about six hours. At one point I looked at the wall above her bed and noticed a painting. The painting struck me as odd, so I looked at it more closely. It was a scene of an African village with a woman nursing a baby at her breast. While doing so, she was cutting her wrist with some sort of ceremonial knife. She was bloodletting and draining the blood into a bowl. The picture was as demonic as they come.

During a brief period when the woman was coherent, I asked her where she had gotten the picture. She told me she had bought it in Africa. I asked her if I could remove it from the apartment and she agreed. I threw the picture out onto the sidewalk, and we proceeded to deal with the numerous demons that were tormenting her.

That was a turning point. We saw significant release in her once the painting was removed. I believe the painting had some sort of hold on this woman; she probably brought a freeloading demon or two home with her from Africa. I wonder how many other people have done the same thing in ignorance.

When I was on a mission trip to south central Mexico a few years ago, Brother David Hogan of Freedom Ministries shared a similar story. He told of a fellow missionary he worked with years earlier who had been buying ornate statues (actually idols) from the local Indians in that region and shipping them to the States as a means to fund his mission's work. This man and Brother David would meet each morning and go to different villages in the jungle to evangelize the people.

One day his fellow missionary did not show up, so Brother David went on without him. This happened for three days. Finally, at the end of the third day, Brother David came out of the jungle early and drove to the man's home. He went up to the door to knock and found it ajar. When Brother Dave entered the home, he saw the missionary and his wife lying unconscious on the floor of their living room. Brother David looked above them to find, on the fireplace mantel, three very ornate idols.

A righteous anger rose up in Brother David. He took the idols out into the yard and beat them into powder with a tire iron. He proceeded to pour diesel fuel over the pile of clay and lit it. As it was burning, the missionary and his wife both came crawling out of their house, choking and gasping for air.

Folks, there is a good reason God says to not take these things into our homes. If you have not done so recently, I recommend you do some housecleaning immediately. Ask the Holy Spirit to assist you, and go through your house from top to bottom, attic to basement. Anything the Holy Spirit shows you to get rid of, get rid of! If you are in doubt, play it safe and get rid of it.

It is amazing to see the things Christians have in their homes. They hold on to demonic objects such as souvenirs, knickknacks and gifts, refusing to let go because "It was Dad's" or "Grandma left it to me." Many people have objects in their homes relating to former love affairs—pictures, jewelry or clothing given to them by a former lover. If you have any article of affection from any love interest other than your spouse, you need to get rid of it. Many people have ungodly CDs, DVDs and videos or, even worse, pornographic movies, books and magazines. The list goes on and on. Ask the Holy Spirit to show you what needs to be removed and be obedient to Him. If you have to, get a Christian friend to help you, but get your house cleaned out.

And not just your house. If any one of these five areas of curses strikes a chord with you in any part of your life, take action. Curses are real, and they will remain an ongoing influence until you deal with them by the blood of Jesus.

Though none of us is yet perfect, it is difficult to move effectively in the deliverance ministry until we have shut the doors to any demonic activity that might have a hold on our own lives. The effects of witchcraft are particularly significant; in fact, the most difficult ministry cases are those involving the sin of witchcraft. We will continue with this topic in the next chapter, discussing some specific areas of involvement. I believe anyone who is involved with these sins has opened himself or herself to the spirit realm and loosed demonic spirits to operate in his or her life.

SEVEN

Seven

Witchcraft and the Occult

I want you to know—I want to make it crystal clear—that *any* involvement with the occult is contrary to God's Word. It is blatant defiance, and it will open a huge door for the devil to come through! Here is one of many Scriptures that show God's clear instructions regarding witchcraft, in this case speaking to the children of Israel:

"When you come into the land which the LORD your God is giving you, you shall not learn to follow the abominations of those nations. There shall not be found among you anyone who makes his son or his daughter pass through the fire, or one who practices witchcraft, or a soothsayer, or one who interprets omens, or a sorcerer, or one who conjures spells, or a medium, or a spiritist, or one who calls up the dead. For all who do these things are an abomination to the LORD, and because of these abominations the LORD your God drives them out from before you. You shall be blameless before the LORD your God. For these nations which you will dispossess

listened to soothsayers and diviners; but as for you, the
LORD your God has not appointed such for you."

Deuteronomy 18:9–14

You may recall the fate of King Saul after he went against
God's law and consulted a medium, hoping through a séance to bring up the prophet Samuel from the dead (see
1 Samuel 28):

> Saul died because he was unfaithful to the LORD; he did not
> keep the word of the LORD and even consulted a medium
> for guidance, and did not inquire of the LORD. So the LORD
> put him to death and turned the kingdom over to David
> son of Jesse.

1 Chronicles 10:13–14, NIV

Many people are naïve about occult involvement because
of its general acceptance and availability. How many folks
have not participated in some "harmless" slumber party
games—Ouija boards, Magic 8-Balls, séances, Bloody Mary,
levitation? We do not realize that these activities are really
invitations to demonic activity in our lives. Levitation, for
instance, is conjuring a demon to come and pick up an
object or carry it around the room. Because the demon is
not visible to the onlookers, it seems as though the conjurer
has great power. As we will see in a moment, the desire for
power is quite a draw into occult activity.

I once heard a story about a private school in Mexico
where the students were playing with a Ouija board. Within
a few minutes more than forty of them were controlled by
demons. They began chewing the legs on the furniture,
growling and foaming at the mouth.

When news about the strange occurrence spread, the
government was called in to investigate. During the course
of their investigation, officials interviewed a top witch in the
region who explained to them the hierarchy of hell in great

detail. She told them about powers and principalities and the hosts of wickedness in the heavenlies. She relayed how demons have territories and rights over people groups in these territories. These children had tapped into the spirit realm, summoned a prince (principality) and had given it a legal right to push out the ruling demon that had been over that region. As an act of appreciation to these children, demons had entered each of them.[1]

Palm reading and tarot cards are not innocent fun either. The same goes for psychics and fortunetellers, who are really mediums. Less understood is the term *familiar spirits*, which we find in Scripture:

> "'Give no regard to mediums and familiar spirits; do not seek after them, to be defiled by them: I am the LORD your God.'"
>
> Leviticus 19:31

> "'And the person who turns to mediums and familiar spirits, to prostitute himself with them, I will set My face against that person and cut him off from his people.'"
>
> Leviticus 20:6

> "'A man or a woman who is a medium, or who has familiar spirits, shall surely be put to death; they shall stone them with stones. Their blood shall be upon them.'"
>
> Leviticus 20:27

Let's take a moment to understand how these spirits work.

Familiar Spirits

I believe we are all assigned an angel and a demon at birth. This statement may sound a bit extreme, but here is my reasoning. We know from Scripture that we have angels assigned to us. Jesus said this to His disciples: "Take heed that you do not despise one of these little ones, for I say to you that in heaven their angels always see the face of My Father who is in heaven" (Matthew 18:10).

And on the other side, we have already noted that Satan counterfeits (or at least tries to counterfeit) everything God does. Thus it seems likely that as far as Satan is able, he commissions demons to keep track of individual human activity. These are what we call familiar spirits.

A familiar or knowing spirit, then, is a spirit that has been assigned to you and has been with you every minute of every day since you were born, taking notes on you and building a case against you. That spirit is not in you, nor is it on you. It is just always with you, observing you and keeping tabs on you. That is why when a person goes to a psychic (who has no real power), the psychic can tell him things about his life that no one knows—no one, that is, except the person himself, God and the demon assigned to that person and his angel! Now the psychic is not a demon; however, he or she is motivated and controlled by a demon. And a good psychic, one who can really read your mind, is more than likely demon-possessed.

Society has become consumed with hunger for the supernatural, making the ancient craft of soothsaying a multi-billion-dollar industry.[2] Products like the Harry Potter books work at desensitizing our children, making witchcraft look not only acceptable but appealing. Truly, though, "there is nothing new under the sun" (Ecclesiastes 1:9). Every new religion, every new cult, every new sect of witchcraft is nothing but an old lie in a new wrapper. In these last days "the devil walks about like a roaring lion, seeking whom he may devour" (1 Peter 5:8).

My wife and I take the spirit realm very seriously. We will not even read a fortune cookie much less a horoscope. Now that may sound fanatical, and I have often been called a fanatic, but when you see the things we have seen, you understand the consequences of even the slightest opening to evil.

I believe familiar spirits not only keep track of us but also direct traffic for other demons to attack us. If someone opens a door in the spirit realm, then whatever demon is available and in the area takes advantage of that open door. The familiar spirit signals that demon and makes him aware of our availability. You see, we are dealing with an enemy who is sophisticated and experienced. He and his demons have been doing this—tormenting humans—for thousands and thousands of years. They are good at it.

Let me share with you a woman's testimony that deals with some of what I have just discussed.

I am 24 years old. Just recently, God set me totally me free. I actually did not know that it could feel this good and that I could feel this close to Jesus and feel His love. I used to think that I was not worth anything, that everybody was going to leave me—that no one really loved me. And even if someone did, that person was just going to hurt me sooner or later. Well, now I know that is not true.

Ever since I was a child, God has had His hand on me. When I was one-and-a-half years old, I was placed on an altar and was about to be sacrificed to the devil, but God intervened. The sacrifice was taking place outside in the woods, and all of a sudden God sent rain, heavy rain, and what looked like headlights all around and a loud noise. Everyone fled. I know now those "lights" were God's angels protecting me.

All this time I have thought God did not love me, but that was just a lie. God had spared my life, and I know for sure that He has a plan for my life. Satan used to tell me that I was useless and that I would never be able to do anything, but that was just a lie, too.

Growing up, I was molested by several men including my uncle, a friend of the family and a neighbor. I thought it was all my fault. As a result, I began looking for love that would not hurt me anymore and that would be there to protect me. At the age of six, I asked a demon (I know that now) to come in and live inside me. I was at a slumber party where we had a séance. A voice said that if I would let it come into me, it would protect me and be my friend. It basically was my comfort, my guide and protector from that moment on. I turned to it for everything.

For the longest time it had a part of my heart. When I got saved, I could not fully feel God's love; it was blocked because I was still holding on to the love and comfort I knew. But just recently, *I was completely set free!* Satan no longer had a part of my heart. Now God could come in and fill my heart with His love.

When God came in, He drove away the fear that had controlled me my whole life. I did not think I could be loved or that I could even love someone. Basically, I could not trust anyone. But Jesus came in and delivered me from all the things that had kept me bound—fear, guilt, shame, satanic rituals, generational curses, rejection, unforgiveness toward myself and others, etc. Jesus came in and healed my heart and filled it with His love. I cannot fully express all that He has done for me. But now I know for sure that Jesus died on the cross for me and His blood washes me clean. It is only through Him that I am free!

I have been through so much and I have seen a lot, but God is a loving God and He forgave everything. He does not remember it anymore. When He looks at me, He sees His child, and a pure, spotless bride.

I mentioned earlier that, in my experience, people who come out of witchcraft backgrounds are the toughest to get free. These cases involving witchcraft will be your hardest cases, but they will also be some of your most rewarding.

I have found two specific areas of witchcraft to be particularly prevalent in deliverance ministry—Wicca and Freemasonry. Let's look at those now.

Wicca

Wicca, claiming its origins to be ancient and mystical, is a religion based on the broad nature and fertility themes of pre-Christian, European paganism. This cult presents itself to the public as a group that focuses on the hidden aspects of nature and its cycles. It uses charms, herbs, chants, circles and candles to commune with nature and one's self.

Wicca is officially recognized by the United States government as a religion. The military has even commissioned Wiccan priests as chaplains in the armed services. These Wiccan priests perform rituals and ceremonies in military and government institutions. Regardless of its benign appearance or status, it is at best a sanitized version of Satan worship.[3]

Wicca is to witchcraft as marijuana is to the drug culture. It is the entry level to Satanism and the occult. Wiccans consider themselves to be "white" witches or, for lack of a better term, "good" witches.

The problem with this is God hates *all* witchcraft; just as there is no distinction in His eyes between "little white lies" and "black lies," so there is no distinction between white witchcraft and black witchcraft. As we noted earlier in Deuteronomy 18:10–12, any type of witchcraft is an abomination to God:

> "Let no one be found among you who sacrifices his son or daughter in the fire, who practices divination or sorcery, interprets omens, engages in witchcraft, or casts spells, or who is a medium or spiritist or who consults the dead. *Anyone who does these things is detestable to the LORD.*"
>
> NIV, emphasis added

God so hates witchcraft that the children of Israel were instructed to kill any witches found among them (see

Exodus 22:18). Paul lists witchcraft among the acts of the sinful nature:

> The acts of the sinful nature are obvious: sexual immorality, impurity and debauchery; idolatry and witchcraft; hatred, discord, jealousy, fits of rage, selfish ambition, dissensions, factions and envy; drunkenness, orgies, and the like. I warn you, as I did before, that *those who live like this will not inherit the kingdom of God.*
>
> Galatians 5:19–21, NIV, emphasis added

The entire chapter of Leviticus 18 consists of warnings to Israel not to adopt the ways of the Canaanites, whose land they were about to enter, or to maintain the ways of the Egyptians, whose land they had just departed from, because both peoples had religions that were steeped in witchcraft. The Canaanites practiced a fertility religion (a root of Wicca, perhaps) that promoted all forms of sexual misconduct and perversion including incest, homosexuality, bestiality, adultery as well as child sacrifice. These abominations were the very reason God was driving the inhabitants from their land.

Modern witchcraft—a term that defines Wicca—is credited to an Englishman named Gerald Gardner who emerged after the British repealed their laws against witchcraft. Gardner wrote several books on the subject, supposedly based on secrets he received from an ancient cult he had been associated with. It is believed he then joined forces with another witch, Doreen Valiente, who helped him develop the tradition known as Gardnerian witchcraft. This combines his own coven's traditions with Rosicrucianism, mythology, Freemasonry and other sources.[4]

Gardnerian witchcraft was introduced to the United States in the 1960s and spread like wildfire across the nation. The counterculture of the late '60s and early '70s was ripe for the attack against societal and Christian values that this sect embraces.

Today several other major traditions with roots in witchcraft are active in this nation: Alexandrian, Druidic, Welsh Traditionalist, Georgian, Dianic and the Church of Wicca,[5] as well as estimated thousands of other small, self-styled cults whose rites and rituals vary to some degree, based on the cult leader's particular brand of lust and perversion. Most of these traditions have a strong emphasis on goddess worship[6] (rooted in the "queen of heaven" mentioned in Jeremiah 7 and 44) and perform rituals to mark natural transitions, such as the lunar phases, equinoxes, solstices and traditional agrarian festivals. Most covens have ceremonies, rites and rituals that include nudity, orgies and other forms of sexual misconduct and perversion. Scourging or whipping, which is nothing more than sadomasochism, and drug use are also a common part of many rituals.

In dealing with any form of witchcraft, including Wicca, the subject of sacrifice and blood sacrifice comes up. Though Wiccans claim not to be involved with any type of animal or human sacrifice, witchcraft has always been associated with the letting of blood. History records Druid and Celtic practices that included both animal and human sacrifice.

The Bible associates human sacrifice, especially child sacrifice, with the activities of witchcraft:

> Manasseh was twelve years old when he became king, and he reigned in Jerusalem fifty-five years. He did evil in the eyes of the LORD, following the detestable practices of the nations the LORD had driven out before the Israelites. He rebuilt the high places his father Hezekiah had demolished; he also erected altars to the Baals and made Asherah poles. He bowed down to all the starry hosts and worshiped them. He built altars in the temple of the LORD, of which the LORD had said, "My Name will remain in Jerusalem forever." In both courts of the temple of the LORD, he built altars to all the starry hosts. *He sacrificed his sons in the fire in the Valley of Ben Hinnom, practiced sorcery, divination and witchcraft, and*

*consulted mediums and spiritists. He did much evil in the eyes
of the LORD, provoking him to anger.*

2 Chronicles 33:1–6, NIV, emphasis added

I found these helpful definitions in an 1828 *Webster's Dictionary*:

> *enchanter:* one who enchants; a sorcerer or magician; one who has spirits or demons at his command; one who practices enchantment, or pretends to perform surprising things by the agency of demons.

> *sorcery:* magic; enchantment; witchcraft; divination by the assistance or supposed assistance of evil spirits, or the power of commanding evil spirits.

> *warlock:* a male witch or wizard.

> *witch:* a woman who, by compact with the devil, practices sorcery or enchantment.

> *witchcraft:* 1: the practice of witches; sorcery; enchantments; intercourse with the devil, 2: power more than natural.

A modern-day Merriam-Webster's dictionary makes this interesting addition:

> *witchcraft:* 1 a: the use of sorcery or magic b: communication with the devil or with a familiar [spirit] 2: an irresistible influence or fascination 3: Wicca.

Another seemingly respectable and acceptable form of witchcraft is called Freemasonry. It is interesting to note that acts performed in witchcraft ceremonies are performed symbolically in Freemasonry ceremonies. Such is the case of the initiation ceremonies, for instance, in which the initiates must be recommended by a current member and be blindfolded, stripped (naked in the witchcraft ceremonies) and led about with nooses around their necks. In both ceremonies, a knife or a sword is placed against the breast of the initiates and a blood oath is made never to tell the secrets of the lodge or coven. In fact, all of the rites of the Masonic lodge are symbols of what is actually performed in witch covens around this nation and the world.

Freemasonry

A number of years ago someone gave me a copy of "Prayers for the Release of Freemasons and Their Descendants" that he had found on the Internet.[7] I read the prayers and found the content to be so bizarre that I filed them away and actually forgot about them.

Months later, my wife and I were ministering to a young woman in the area of deliverance and not getting anywhere. One day the woman said she felt as though she had curses on her from her father. Her father was the Grand something or other of a Masonic lodge and had molested her as a young girl. She also remembered that her father had said things over her, maybe some kind of prayers or chants. I told her about the prayers I had read for release from Freemasonry, but mentioned the bizarre content. This woman was so desperate to be free she was willing to try anything.

I dug out the prayers and studied them again. They were still weird. After studying the prayers some more, I went out and got a book on Freemasonry. As I began to read, I started to see the specific spirits behind Freemasonry: the spirits of Antichrist, bondage, witchcraft, error, infirmity and perversion. I then decided to give the prayers a try at our next session.

As the young woman began praying the prayers, she started to yawn and cough and manifest in various ways. In about an hour and a half she was set free—I mean *so* free! We were all amazed and pleasantly surprised by the results of praying deliverance prayers related to Freemasonry.

Ever since that episode I have begun to ask the people I minister to if they have any Freemasonry in their backgrounds. If they do, I lead them through the prayers, renouncing the strongholds and manifestations of Freemasonry, and the Holy Spirit brings incredible freedom to their lives. I am continually amazed at testimony after testimony telling of the awesome deliverance and healing people have received by being set free from Freemasonry.[8]

While leading people through deliverance, I have found distinct patterns associated with people who have Masonic backgrounds. I have noticed almost without exception that women whose parents or grandparents (but more often grandparents) were involved in Freemasonry had been molested as children. In most cases they were violated by a close family member, but if not by a family member then by a family friend, a babysitter, a schoolteacher or even a pastor or priest. I truly cannot tell you the overwhelming number of horrible, nasty stories of perversion, molestation, rape and incest I have heard. It is astounding.

Another pattern involving Freemasonry is a spirit of infirmity, which manifests primarily as breathing or lung disorders; asthma and allergies are the most prevalent. I once had a deliverance team member who prayed the prayers quietly while I was leading another person through them. She felt something lift physically off her shoulders and was set free from a lifelong asthma condition.

There is a host of other manifestations and fruits we can attribute directly to Freemasonry, including gallbladder problems, intestinal disorders, female problems and cancers. People's emotions are often heavily affected as well, especially in the areas of anger and fear.

History of Freemasonry

Freemasons claim their spiritual ancestry back to Solomon's Temple and its builder, who they claim was a man named Hiram Abiff. The rites, rituals and worship, as well as the statues and icons of the various lodges, actually date back to ancient Egypt. Freemasonry's documented history, however, begins in the year 1717 with a lodge in London, England.[9]

Freemasonry purports to be a Christian organization; it is amazing to look through a Masonic Bible and to see so much "mixing of the holy with the profane." Masons include the Holy Bible in their rituals and ceremonies, but they also use the Koran, the Hindu "Vedas" and the Laws of Confucius, if the initiate's religious beliefs so dictate. In other areas of the world, they use the writings of whatever religion is popular in that particular culture. That is, of course, a far cry from Christian orthodoxy.

Freemasonry also presents itself as a fraternal organization that does good deeds for the community, particularly widows and orphans. It also supports hospitals and gives scholarships to students. These and many other acts seem virtuous.

The problem comes, however, from the fact that doing these good works is based on one of the biggest and most deceptive lies of Freemasonry, which is this: "Man is not sinful, but merely imperfect. He can, therefore, redeem himself through good works." This negates the redemptive work of Jesus Christ on the cross of Calvary. In fact, Masonic rites and rituals not only negate Jesus' death, burial and resurrection but actually mock Jesus, His sacrificial death and the sacred ordinances of the Church. Freemasonry is a religion that embraces all other religions and every type of witchcraft.

Basic Structure, Rites and Rituals

The Masonic lodge has two basic divisions. The first is the blue lodge, where the first three degrees are earned.

These are the most common lodges and can be found in almost any town throughout the nation. Once a person achieves the third, or Master Mason Degree, he moves to the next division, either the York Rite or the Scottish Rite. After reaching the thirty-second degree, he is eligible to become a Shriner. The thirty-third degree can be earned or it can be honorary. Some presidents and other influential people have been given honorary thirty-third degrees for public relations reasons. It is the belief of Freemasons that each degree earned brings them closer to "light" and to enlightenment. Sadly, however, deception is a key ingredient in Freemasonry; the initiate never really knows the truth.

According to the man considered to be the father of modern Freemasonry, Albert Pike, this deception is intentional. He wrote his epic *Morals and Dogma of the Ancient and Accepted Scottish Rite of Freemasonry* in 1871 after spending much time studying the Hindu "Vedas," which are said to be written so as to prevent their being understood.[10]

Here is a quote from *Morals and Dogma*:

> Masonry, like all the Religions, all the Mysteries, Hermeticism and Alchemy, conceals its secrets from all except the Adepts and Sages, or the Elect, and uses false explanations and misinterpretations of its symbols to mislead those who deserve only to be misled; to conceal the Truth, which it calls Light, from them, and to draw them away from it. Truth is not for those who are unworthy or unable to receive it, or would pervert it. So God Himself incapacitates many men, by color-blindness, to distinguish colors, and leads the masses away from the highest Truth, giving them the power to attain only so much of it as it is profitable to them to know. Every age has had a religion suited to its capacity.[11]

He also immersed himself in the study of the cultic teachings and witchcraft of the French lodge, which was so demonic and steeped in witchcraft that English and American lodges had boycotted it since 1765.[12] After studying the

French lodge, Pike later wrote a six-volume work containing 1,460 pages discussing its practices. He then used these writings, which are considered to be radically anti-Christian and cultic in nature, to redesign the fourth through thirty-third degrees of the Scottish Rite.[13]

Pike was also known to be a Luciferian and heavily involved in magic and astrology. He spent considerable time studying Jewish Kabala (Jewish mysticism), which may have contributed to his frequent bouts of depression and seclusion.[14]

I want to make a personal observation here. Everyone we have ever ministered to who has been heavily involved with witchcraft and the occult has battled severe depression and suicidal thoughts, often with some form of self-mutilation. I do not find it strange, therefore, that Albert Pike also dealt with them. Trees produce fruit; a good tree produces good fruit and a bad tree produces bad fruit.

The following is another quote from Albert Pike, made during his time as the Sovereign Grand Commander of the Supreme Council of the Grand Sovereign Inspectors General of the Thirty-third Degree:

> That which we say to a crowd is, we worship a God, but it is the God one adores without superstition. To you, Sovereign Grand Inspectors General, we say this, that you may repeat it to the Brethren of the thirty-second, thirty-first, and the thirtieth degrees: The Masonic Religion should be, by all of us initiates of the high degrees, maintained in the purity of the Luciferian Doctrine. . . . Yes, Lucifer is God, and unfortunately Adonay is also God. . . . Thus the doctrine of Satanism is heresy. . . . Lucifer, God of Light and God of Good, is struggling for humanity against Adonay, God of Darkness and Evil.[15]

If nothing else were known about Freemasonry, this would suffice to prove that it is demonic. Since many people seeking deliverance ministry have some connection with

Freemasonry, however, I want you to have a broader understanding of the rituals and how they affect the initiates and their families to the third, fourth and even the tenth generations.

The deceptive nature of Freemasonry begins with induction into the lodge. When a member of the lodge wants to recruit a new member, he does not ask that person to join. Instead, he has his wife go to that person's wife who, in turn, persuades her husband to ask the member about the lodge. If the man is single, a close female friend of his will be approached. This gives the devil a legal right to torment that person, because he opened the door himself by asking about membership in the lodge.

After a man joins the lodge, he must go through an initiation ceremony. In the ceremony, he is stripped to the waist and blindfolded, and a noose is placed around his neck. (The spirit of infirmity comes in from the noose around the neck, which is shown by the fruit of asthma, allergies and other breathing disorders.) He is then taken outside the lodge and told to knock on the lodge door. The person who answers the door asks the initiate what he wants, and the initiate responds with these words, "I want to come out of the darkness and enter into the light of Freemasonry."

As the ceremony continues, the initiate is brought back into the lodge, still blindfolded, and a dagger or sword or other sharp object is placed against his bare chest. He then swears the first of many blood oaths and curses over himself and his family, agreeing to be murdered or mutilated if the oath of the degree is violated.

During this first or "entered apprentice" degree, the Worshipful Master of the lodge lays his hands on the initiate and dedicates him to the God of the lodge (which you now know is Lucifer). He also asks that "by the secrets of our art or craft he [the initiate] may gain eternal life."

In the ceremony to obtain the third degree, the initiate is again blindfolded and led around by a noose around his neck.

The initiate is then approached by three ruffians who demand the initiate tell them the secrets of Freemasonry. The person leading the initiate around answers for him, refusing to tell the three ruffians the secrets. They then proceed symbolically to beat the initiate to death and place him into a coffin or on a stretcher as a symbolic burial. This, by the way, invites in a spirit of death to the initiate and his family. After some time passes, the Worshipful Master of the lodge directs a man wearing a glove that resembles a lion's paw to reach down and pull the initiate out of the darkness of death and into the light of Freemasonry. This ritual is an absolute mockery of the death, burial and resurrection of Jesus Christ.

In the ritual of the eighteenth degree, and in other degrees, the initiate takes part in a false communion that includes a biscuit, salt and white wine. In many false communions the wine is drunk from a human skull. This, again, is an abomination and an absolute mockery of Jesus Christ and the sacrament of Holy Communion.

In the higher degrees of Freemasonry, initiates proclaim Lucifer to be God. They also invoke a wide variety of gods and goddesses, including Egyptian and Hindu deities. The Shriners plainly proclaim Allah to be God. Have you ever driven by a Shriners' temple? Look at one sometime: It is nothing more than an Islamic mosque.

The principal spirit behind Freemasonry is witchcraft. The Masons have drawn from every type of witchcraft, including Kabala, Rosicrucianism and the occult, in an effort to gain power, which I truly believe they are trying to use as a means to control the rest of mankind. Once the door is opened and the enemy has been given a legal right, his attack will be relentless until he gets his due. He will use anyone and anything to accomplish his plan.

Wicca, Freemasonry and all other forms of witchcraft are about control of others to fulfill one's own desires. They are about gaining power to have one's own way, and God hates that.

Eight

Satanic Ritual Abuse and Multiple Personality Disorder

Any comprehensive teaching on deliverance would be incomplete without a section dedicated to the horrors of satanic ritual abuse (SRA)[1] and the consequence faced by its victims/survivors known as multiple personality disorder (MPD)[2]. In fact, if you are in the deliverance ministry, you may have already had some dealings with MPD and may not even have known it. (Definitions for these and other terms throughout this chapter can be found in the endnotes.)

Actually, the deliverance ministry at Brownsville Revival School of Ministry was founded as a means to minister to a girl who had MPD and who was also a survivor of SRA. Since then our teams have ministered to numerous other SRA victims, many of whom have had some form of personality disorder.

This chapter is by no means an all-inclusive teaching on this complex subject. In fact, it is just an introduction to it. My desire is to make you aware of it, enable you to recognize it and show you how it opens doors to the enemy. It is up to you to decide if you are ready, willing and able to deal with it. This chapter will focus on four main areas that are vital to understand when ministering to a person in the areas of SRA and MPD:

1. The truth about SRA.
2. What MPD is and is not.
3. How to recognize MPD.
4. How to minister effectively to someone with MPD.

The Truth about Satanic Ritual Abuse

Ministering to SRA victims and persons with personality disorders is another controversial area of the deliverance ministry. Very few people understand the reality of these horrors and, therefore, do not see the need for this type of ministry. Many others are confused by it and, as a result, want no involvement with it. Many are also afraid of possible legal consequences that could arise from dealing with it.

As I look into human history, I am continually amazed at "man's inhumanity to his fellow man." Even in biblical accounts we read of invading armies butchering innocent men, women and children. There are accounts of men ripping open the bellies of pregnant women and dashing infants against the rocks. Today the practice of abortion takes the lives of millions upon millions of children. Partial birth abortions have become legal, allowing for the bodies of these aborted infants to be butchered (harvested) and sold for various medical and commercial uses.

Satanic ritual abuse is perhaps the most horrific, inhumane atrocity practiced by man throughout the ages. The

Bible is rich with accounts of not only satanic worship but also of child sacrifice and satanic ritual abuse:

> "You shall not worship the LORD your God in that way; for every abomination to the LORD which He hates they have done to their gods; for they burn even their sons and daughters in the fire to their gods."
>
> Deuteronomy 12:31

> They even sacrificed their sons and their daughters to demons, and shed innocent blood, the blood of their sons and daughters, whom they sacrificed to the idols of Canaan; and the land was polluted with blood. Thus they were defiled by their own works, and played the harlot by their own deeds.
>
> Psalm 106:37–39

The first quote is God's warning to the children of Israel not to practice the evil ways of the people of the land they were about to inhabit. The second quote is a description of how God's own people did not heed His warning and learned to serve the idols of the Gentiles. The practices describe ritual child sacrifice and infanticide.

So why is it that reports of ritual child abuse and satanic ritual abuse surprise people today? In fact, the world for the most part denies not only satanic ritual abuse but even the existence of Satan himself.[3] Satan has done an excellent job of disguising himself and his works in this modern age.

What Is Multiple Personality Disorder?

Let me begin by stating that not all people with MPD are victims of satanic ritual abuse. I have worked with some cases in which the person had been severely and cruelly abused, but no traces of Satanism or even ritualistic abuse were ever discovered. In one instance (and only one instance), the girl I was working with had not been sexually abused at all.

In the other cases I have dealt with, however, not only have the persons been sexually abused, but all but one had been abused by their fathers. In the one case in which the person was not a victim of sexual abuse, she had experienced severe verbal abuse as well as some physical abuse from her parents. We found her to be extremely sensitive, being easily upset by the slightest thing. The best I can figure is that the verbal abuse she received was as damaging to her as sexual abuse would have been to someone else. I often note that what devastates one person may have little or no effect on another. Remember, each individual is unique.

In the case of SRA, multiple personality disorder is not only a somewhat natural result of this extreme abuse, but it is also believed to be intentionally inflicted on its victims for three apparent reasons:

1. Child victims, if not killed in a ritual sacrifice, might tell someone what happened to them or what they have seen in the rituals. In order to protect the cult/coven, therefore, the child is subjected to ritual torture with the intention of fragmenting their minds and creating alters[4] or fragmented personalities.
2. If and when these persons escape the group at some later date and are saved, deliverance and inner healing is a long and tedious process at best.
3. These children are programmed[5] to a certain degree in order to maintain control over them and to keep them loyal to the leaders.

MPD is a seemingly normal human behavior or reaction to an abnormal situation or circumstance. It is *not* a sickness or a disease or a mental illness.[6] It is the natural reaction of young children to severe physical, sexual, mental or verbal abuse (including torture or brainwashing) in which they cannot escape physically from the situation so they escape mentally. Let me give you a hypothetical example.

Little Mary is four years old and her father, or some other adult male, rapes or molests her, tortures her, and threatens to kill her or her mommy if she tells anyone. Little Mary cannot cope with the results of the abuse, the pain, the humiliation and the terror she is experiencing. Therefore, she decides in her little mind that nothing ever happened to her and she disassociates[7] or separates herself from the memory by creating a separate little girl or boy personality (yes, many female SRA victims will take on little boy personalities, often thinking, *If I were a boy this would not be happening to me*).[8] Also, later in life, a young woman may find herself in a lesbian relationship and take on a male personality in order to deal with that situation.

Regardless of the child's sex, the "new" personality can deal with the trauma, so it is as if nothing ever happened to the child who is being abused (the host.)[9]

This phenomenon of *disassociation* is defined by *The Diagnostic Manual of the American Psychiatric Association* as "a disturbance or alteration in the normal integrative function of memory, identity or consciousness." The psychiatric community has recently relabeled MPD as *dissociative identity disorder* (DID)[10] in an attempt to explain what actually takes place in a person during disassociation.

In some cases one alter is created to deal with a recurring trauma. In other cases several alters are created to handle one particular experience; the trauma is so severe that numerous alters are required to deal with it. Each alter, or altered personality state, has a different name and age according to the specific trauma or part of a trauma that it is associated with. I have seen as many as 118 personalities in one individual.

In one young woman we found sixteen four-year-old al-ters who had all come about during one satanic ritual. They all said they "were married to an angel named Lucifer." A couple of the alters described Lucifer as a "pretty man." Several went on to explain how he had lain on them and hurt them so badly that they could not bear the pain, so another alter came and took some of the pain away.

Once people are accustomed to splitting or fragment-ing their minds, they can and often will develop alters as a way to deal with many of life's problems. This occurs in later years, too, well after the childhood abuse has ceased. Altered personalities may be utilized to handle difficult situations with boyfriends, marital problems, jobs, acci-dents, the death of a loved one or any unpleasant task or difficult situation.[11]

I ministered to one woman who had been a stripper. When she performed at a strip club, her alter would take over and she would become that person, using the alter's name as her stage name. She had different personalities for every aspect of her life because it was easier for her to split off into a new person than deal with any of life's stresses.

Please note that alters are not demons. Some people be-lieve that all alters are demons. I do not agree with this theory at all. I believe alters would be better described as imaginary friends called upon to help people when they cannot help themselves or deal with whatever may be going on at the time. Alters can, however, and oftentimes do have demons that need to be cast out of them. And demons will sometimes disguise themselves as alters in hopes of not being discovered and cast out.

There is a lot of good information on MPD/DID found in various books and on the Internet. Be aware, of course, that the secular medical and psychological worlds discount the spiritual aspect of MPD and exclude the demonic altogether. Also note that most of the non-technical material is so de-scriptive of the abuse done to the victims that it borders, if not crosses, the line of pornographic reading. This is another area, like all areas of the supernatural, where we need to guard ourselves against fascination and seduction.

The best resource I have found on this subject is James G. Friesen's groundbreaking book *Uncovering the Mystery of MPD*.[12] In fact, I would recommend not attempting to minister in this area at all until reading this book. James Friesen, a Christian psychologist, really pioneered this ministry. There are also two nonprofit organizations that can provide you with much good information. They are the Sidran Institute, found on the Internet at www.sidran.org, and the International Society for the Study of Dissociation, found at www.issd.org. Aside from my personal experiences, much of my research for this chapter comes from these three sources.

Before you go any further, I would like to recommend that you go to the endnotes for this chapter and read the definitions of the words used in connection with personality disorders if you have not already done so. This will help you as much as anything in understanding this phenomenon.

How to Recognize Multiple Personality Disorder

How can you tell if the person you are dealing with has a multiple personality disorder? If you are working with a person who is just not getting free, MPD may at least be a consideration.

In one case, as we were working our way through a deliverance session using our ministry's *Deliverance Training Manual*,[13] we came to the area of a deaf and dumb spirit. I began to look over the page, and the word MPD jumped out at me. I asked the woman we were ministering to if she had ever been diagnosed with MPD. She replied that she had indeed been diagnosed as having that disorder. I asked her why she had not told me, and she said she was afraid to. She feared that we might not have ministered to her had we known.

In another case we cast the same demon out three weeks in a row. Finally I prayed and asked God what was going on, and He answered clearly: *She has MPD; therefore, you are casting the same demon out of each personality.*

If you are ministering to a person and suspect MPD or if the ministry process has just come to a standstill, I suggest you ask the following questions. These questions may help you determine if the person you are working with has some type of personality disorder such as MPD or borderline personality disorder (BPD).[14]

1. Do you lose part of your day? Or lose track of time? Do you find yourself driving and suddenly realize you do not know where you are or where you have been or where you are going?
2. Do you have childlike states where you feel like or act like a little girl?[15]
3. Do you have visions or flashbacks[16] or hallucinations that frighten or torment you? Are they recurring? What is their nature? (If they involve rape, molestation, witchcraft or themes consistent with satanic ritual abuse or severe child abuse, they may indicate MPD.)
4. Do you hear voices in your head? Do they seem to argue with each other?
5. Do you often feel as though you do not know who you are?
6. Do you remember your childhood? (If the person does not have memory before age six or seven, or if he says he does not remember it at all, or even if he says "I think it was happy," there is a strong possibility of MPD.)
7. Do you ever find yourself dressed totally different from normal, or discover that your hairstyle and makeup are totally different?

8. Growing up did you feel like a sex addict, always having an abnormally strong sexual curiosity or sexual desires?
9. Do you feel or have you in the past felt you are a witch? Do you think you are a witch?
10. Do you feel as though you have deep inward pain without any memories to justify the pain?

These all could be signs of some degree or some form of a personality disorder. If a large percentage of these is present, you are very possibly dealing with MPD, DID or BPD. Other indications of personality disorders can include eating disorders; self-mutilation such as cutting, beating and hair pulling; severe mood swings; panic attacks; suicidal thoughts, as well as actual attempts; sexual assaults by incubus or succubus demons; body memories;[17] and other bizarre behavior. And remember, if a person goes through deliverance continually but never gets free, or only experiences freedom for short periods of time before all his or her symptoms reappear, you are probably dealing with MPD or at least BPD.

Ministering to Someone with MPD

If you suspect that someone who has come to you for ministry has multiple personality disorder, be advised: If you are not an experienced counselor or deliverance minister, seek competent professional or ministerial help for the person in need. This is not a time for experimentation on your part. For your own training, find deliverance ministers whom you know to bear good fruit and ask if you might enter under their tutelage. Do not take a chance on causing harm to the person seeking ministry and opening yourself to legal action.

If you are qualified in the field of deliverance ministry and suspect that you are ministering to a case or cases of MPD, here are some guidelines that might assist you.

Be direct with the individuals regarding the possibility of MPD but not leading. Never say, "I think you have multiple personality disorder." I generally ask them if they know what MPD is. Prior to this stage I have obtained significant information about them, including, assuming they have revealed it, whether or not they have been in a mental institution or under psychiatric care. If they have, I ask if they have ever been diagnosed with MPD. I then explain the different types of personality disorders and the symptoms. The ideal situation is for them to suggest that maybe they have a personality disorder.

After establishing the possibility of a personality disorder, I then ask for their permission to try something. Since the individuals with MPD are predominately women, I then say something like this: "I would like to speak to the little girl who would like to speak to me. I would like you to come up and talk to me."

It is amazing to watch as their facial expressions change and their eyes blink as they switch personalities[18] on you. Suddenly you find yourself talking with a two-year-old or a four-year-old girl who most often, but not always, uses a little girl voice and mannerisms.

I then proceed to ask this personality her name, age, if she is the host's (person you are ministering to) friend, and if she came to help this person. I also ask each alter if he or she would like to help me help[19] the host. I then ask why she came in to help and what happened to make the host need her. Oftentimes the alter proceeds with a graphic description of a ritualistic ceremony including rape, molestation, bestiality, murder, cannibalism, infanticide or other atrocities.

At this point I make sure one of my team members is taking detailed notes (by detailed I mean "he said-she said" type notes). This will help you later to track the personalities or map[20] the person's system.[21] Sometimes the person you are working with will later question what was said by the alters or by you. I was in the insurance business for almost fourteen years and saw a lot of claim disputes, legal threats and lawsuits. I have found that good notes make a tremendous difference to attorneys, judges and family members. Likewise in ministry, detailed notes can clarify any questions later. Lawsuits related to deliverance ministry are not at all uncommon.

When speaking to alters, I try to gather as much information as I can, including which other alters they know, their ages, who hurt them, where they were at the time they were hurt and any other pertinent information I can obtain.[22]

I then end the session with enough time to discuss the findings with the person we are ministering to, as well as with my team members, especially if they have not previously worked with MPD.

Several things need to be addressed at this point with the persons you are ministering to. You need to ask them what they think about MPD and about the abuses described by the alters. After the hosts hear everything that was said, you then need to minister to or counsel them accordingly. People generally respond with comments such as, "Well, now this or that makes sense" or "That explains a lot" or "Well, I am not crazy after all." But oftentimes the response is not as positive, and you have a very upset individual weeping and asking you, "Am I crazy?" or "Is this real?" or "I don't remember those things ever happening to me." This can be a very sensitive and difficult time for the host and you. You will need great patience, understanding and compassion as you explain what MPD is—in particular that it is not a mental illness but rather a coping mechanism used to deal with the trauma they otherwise might not have survived.

I explain to them that our brains are incredibly powerful; the average person only uses about 5 percent of it. MPD probably saved them from going crazy by helping them deal with the traumas just revealed. I also tell them that

I believe the ability of the mind to fragment or split like this is a gift from God. Instead of fretting or being upset, they need to start thanking God for giving them the intelligence to be a multiple. I use an analogy of a large server or mainframe computer and the networking of numerous PCs. I explain to them that they are like the mainframe and their alters are like the PCs. Only a person with very high intelligence is capable of managing all that.

I also tell them that I do not believe God would have brought this to light now unless they were able to bear it now. As children they could not bear it; that is why their minds fragmented. But now they are saved, older and more mature. They can now handle the truth. And the truth will set them so free!

At this point, it is important to obtain what secular psychotherapy calls "informed consent."[23] Informed consent involves full disclosure to the persons receiving ministry of the problem as you see it, the manner in which you intend to proceed in ministry, the risks and benefits of continuing to be ministered to, and the likely outcome with and without ministry. The information must be presented in a way that the persons understand. They must then decide whether or not to continue with ministry.

If the individuals are married, I insist on sharing all of the above information and obtaining that same "informed consent" from their spouses. (After all, the spouse is the one who will be living with the person through all the difficulties in the next few weeks, months or even years.) The spouse will need much patience and understanding, and will be instrumental in the person's healing. Often the spouse expresses relief upon learning that there is a reason for all the hell that has been in their marriage and their home.

I once dealt with a woman who has struggled with deliverance issues for years and has never felt totally free. Once the possibility of MPD was discovered, I wanted her to know the pros and cons of proceeding or stopping at that particular point in the deliverance process. We had been ministering to her for several months, and she had a good degree of freedom. In fact, she was probably experiencing more freedom at that point than she had ever experienced in her entire life. She was still experiencing pain, however, without memories of the cause. I drew her a graph. I labeled one end "mild dissociation," such as daydreaming, and the other end "full-blown MPD" with a large number of personalities. In the middle there was BPD. I explained to her where I thought she was on this scale.

I then drew her another chart, which I called a "pain graph." I asked her to mark on the chart where her pain level was when she first came to me for deliverance. Then I had her mark her current level of pain. She had come to me with pain level averaging a seven on the scale, but often going up to a ten. She said now her pain ranged from zero to three on an average day. I then extended the graph we started with (ranging from zero to ten) to fifteen.

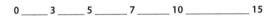

0 _____ 3 _____ 5 _____ 7 _____ 10 _____ 15

I then explained to her that when you start dealing with MPD, when you open it up, so to speak, you start learning about things that happened to you often by family members. Your pain level will often shoot up to a fifteen or above. I also shared the fact that if we continued to proceed with the deliverence process, it could literally be years before she got back to the level of low pain she was enjoying right then.

She asked a legitimate question at that point. She asked, "Will I always have to live with the pain?" I shared a story with her about my back. I had injured it many years ago and had to be in traction for about a week. I then had to be in physical therapy for almost a year. My back is now in pretty good shape, but the pain still flares up from time to time. It probably has soreness in it more often than not. In spite of that little bit of pain and discomfort, I function well. I minister and basically do anything I want to do or the Lord wants me to do. She, likewise, could possibly continue to function at her low level of pain. But she had a further option: She could eventually, with hard work, be free of pain altogether.

By use of the two charts and answering her questions, I believe I fulfilled all reasonable "informed consent" requirements. She chose to stop all ministry for the time being and enjoy her newfound freedom. We did agree that if she wanted additional ministry in the future we would provide it. Several years have now passed, and I saw her recently at a conference. She had an absolute glow on her face. She was still enjoying the freedom she received.

If these individuals decide to continue in counseling and deliverance ministry, it is important to express a few cautions to them.

> First, these individuals should be very careful about sharing any personal information regarding MPD. Most people do not understand MPD and may give poor counsel, shun them, tell them they are crazy or in some other way inflict even more pain on them.
>
> Second, they should not read anything on MPD or SRA that you have not given them or recommended to them. A multitude of materials is available on the Internet and on the shelves of just about every bookstore. Caution them that some materials could pollute or contaminate their minds or memories; other people's accounts of abuse could possibly create false memories;[24] some secular material could confuse or disturb them.
>
> Third, if they are currently involved in any kind of ministry, I recommend they take a sabbatical. They are going to spend an indefinite period of time dealing

with wounds and hurts from their past that they never knew of before, and there are going to be some difficult times ahead.

The next step is to refer the person to a local physician. We were blessed in Pensacola to have several Christian doctors available. It is important to have a licensed medical doctor confirm your suspicion and give an official diagnosis as to whether or not the individual has MPD/DID or BPD. This corroboration is vital if the person is going to continue receiving ministry. Plus, it avoids the appearance of your practicing medicine without a license.

If you are going to continue leading the person through deliverance and counseling, it is important that you understand some of the issues that may come up.

Secular therapists suggest that most MPD patients digress during therapy; they often get worse before they get better. But therapists agree that they can be restored to health after all of the abusive memories are uncovered and all the alters are merged into the host personality.

There may be periods of denial where the patients refuse to believe what the alters are saying. Once they finally deal with the reality of it, they may go through periods of grief, anger, rage, fear and other emotions they never had to deal with before. As a result, they are at times going to be a mess. They may also deal with severe bouts of depression and anxiety.

There may be spirits of suicide at work. I have read that as many as 72 percent of people with MPD attempt suicide. I am not sure if this statistic was before or after diagnosis; I assume it was after. In any case we need to be aware of the risk of suicide. (Remember, this person is without a doubt demonized to some degree.) Some therapists believe that where programming is involved, there may be specific destroyer demons involved that will try to kill them or cause them to kill themselves.[25]

These individuals will also have forgiveness issues to deal with as they discover how loved ones and people who were supposed to care for them did unspeakable things to them. They will discover not only that they were tortured, raped and forced to take part in horrible rituals, but they were also lied to and deceived all of their lives. In essence, their whole lives have been a lie!

As you start dealing with the altered personalities, you will find some friendly alters, some hostile or bad alters, as well as many in between. Some will not trust you for a while; you will have to earn their trust. Remember, every other person whom the alters have trusted up until now has probably abused or violated them.

If you do choose to minister to people with MPD or other types of personality disorders, you need to expect a lengthy ordeal. One of our teams ministered to one girl, one or more sessions per week, for seventeen months. In another instance, we worked with the person for fourteen months. In another, twelve months. (The latter two we ended up referring to a Christian psychologist for treatment.)

On the other hand, we have had numerous cases that lasted from two to six months and had outstanding results, especially with some of the older women. I attribute this to the fact that they were older in the Lord and more grounded in the Word. This helped them be better equipped to deal with the realities that were uncovered. In any case involving MPD/DID or BPD, there are a lot of uncertainties and variables; time is definitely one of them.

Nine

Emotional Wounding

The final point of entry for demonic activity that we will consider is the open door that comes from emotional injury and hurts, including rejection, abandonment and abuse. As we will see in part 3, emotional wounding can be dealt with effectively through the ministries of deliverance and inner healing.

As with the subject of demonic activity itself, we also see people generally taking one of two extreme viewpoints regarding this subject. Some say, "Forget the past. Don't bring it up. Let it rest." They explain: "Too many people blame their problems on their pasts. All they need to do is grow up and get over it."

Others feel just the opposite. They believe that every problem in the present can be linked to and blamed on a past issue. They say, "I can't help being this way; I had a rough upbringing. It's not my fault that I get angry or impatient."

I believe, again, that the truth is always somewhere in the middle. It is necessary to deal with past issues and hurts in order to gain full healing, but our pasts cannot be used to excuse wrong behavior patterns, attitudes or actions.

A past hurt is like a festering sore on your body. Although a scab may cover it, underneath it can still be full of infection and pus; it is just a nasty mess. At some point, therefore, we must pull off the scab and clean out the wound. Then and only then will it heal properly and the pain leave.

Inner healing is just as much a part of deliverance as is casting out demons. In many cases, it is the main pathway to freedom. It uncovers the wounds in one's soul, which allows the Holy Spirit to come in and pour His healing balm on them.

There are many terms used to describe inner healing, terms like soul healing, healing of memories, Theophostic healing and numerous others. Regardless of what we call it, we need to understand that unhealed hurts do hinder our Christian walk. The devil will use every opportunity to cause us harm or damage. If we allow an open door through hurts, then he will take full advantage of it.

We have all experienced hurts along the way, and we have all dealt with them differently. As I stated earlier, what hurt me terribly might not have affected you at all, and what devastated you might not have bothered me as much. Regardless, I know that it is God's will that we be totally healed of all hurts and be free to serve Him unhindered by our pasts.

The following is a list of questions that may indicate wounds and/or emotional hurts:

1. Do you struggle with irrational behavior at times?
2. Do you struggle with fears that grip you and almost overpower you at times?
3. Do you have moments when anger and rage well up within you?
4. Do you have strong feelings of inferiority, low self-esteem or insecurity?
5. Do you have practically uncontrollable appetites?

6. Do you have a critical spirit or a judgmental spirit?
7. Do you have a problem with jealousy?
8. Do you battle continually with depression?
9. Do you have a restless or nervous nature?
10. Are you a perfectionist or do you struggle with compulsive behaviors?
11. Do you feel hopelessness and despair?[1]

Answering yes to any of these questions may indicate some deep inner hurts that need inner healing. I always tell folks that God, through His Holy Spirit, is the only one who can heal their hurts. He made you, and He can fix you!

Isaiah 61:1, which Jesus read aloud to those gathered in a synagogue at the opening of His ministry, states:

"The Spirit of the Lord GOD is upon Me, because the LORD has anointed Me to preach good tidings to the poor; He has sent Me to heal the brokenhearted, to proclaim liberty to the captives, and the opening of the prison to those who are bound."

As Christ's followers we must bring healing to the brokenhearted and proclaim liberty to the captives. The deliverance ministry is often thought of as a ministry involving only intense warfare; in reality, it is a ministry displaying the character of God through great love and compassion. Acts 10:38 speaks of how Jesus went about doing good and healing all who were oppressed of the devil; He focused on the goodness and the character of God, and He set people free.

When we are born again, our spirits are the only part of us that is changed. Our souls (meaning our minds, wills and emotions) and our bodies remain unchanged at salvation. This means that our souls and bodies must go through a process of healing and restoration called *sanctification*. Inner healing is a vital part of that process. It can, however, be a lengthy part of the process as each layer of hurts is exposed and cleaned up until we are completely whole. Yet we can rest assured that if we let Him, God will bring us safely through and make us completely whole in spirit, soul and body:

> Now may the God of peace Himself sanctify you completely; and may your whole spirit, soul, and body be preserved blameless at the coming of our Lord Jesus Christ. He who calls you is faithful, who also will do it.
>
> 1 Thessalonians 5:23–24

Deliverance and inner healing go hand in hand to get a person set totally free. Suppose, for instance, that someone has been stabbed by a knife. Pulling the knife out would be comparable to deliverance. But the resulting wound would still need time to heal. It might also need some special attention—bandages or stitches. That process is not unlike inner healing.

The Fruit of Depression

One of the most common fruits of deep inner hurts is depression. I believe the devil uses depression against us so mercilessly because he knows that if he can cause a person to be depressed and discouraged, it will render his or her entire being powerless. Look at these verses: "A merry heart makes a cheerful countenance, but by sorrow of the heart the spirit is broken [wounded]" (Proverbs 15:13); "A merry heart does good, like medicine, but a broken spirit dries the bones" (Proverbs 17:22); "The spirit of a man will sustain him in sickness, but who can bear a broken spirit?" (Proverbs 18:14).

According to the National Institute of Mental Health, 35 million Americans (more than 16 percent of the population) suffer from depression severe enough to warrant treatment at some time in their lives.[2] We spend billions of dollars on medical care and work-related absenteeism and lost productivity due to depression and anxiety. The emotional costs are even more staggering—broken marriages, troubled children, suicides, homicides. Depression is the oldest known psychiatric disorder, but scientists still do not know entirely what causes it, much less why most of its victims are women.[3] Without the Holy Spirit's divine revelation, they will never figure it out because it is a spiritual matter and most, if not all, is rooted in deep inner hurts and rejection. We see a biblical account of depression in 1 Samuel 15–16. King Saul lost his anointing as Israel's king because of his disobedience to God, though he still sat on the throne. Aware of his sin and rebellion and loss, King Saul was often attacked by heaviness and depression. Whenever he was distressed he would call on David to play anointed psalms, which would drive the spirits away and cause the depression to lift.

The Children's Plight

All of us are subject to hurts at all ages and at all points of our lives. For some reason it seems that a lot of traumatic hurts and attacks—and maybe even the most tragic—come against children by the age of two. As I pondered this one day, my wife brought to my attention how Satan tried to kill the babies during Moses' day in Egypt. Scripture records Pharaoh's decree:

> Then the king of Egypt spoke to the Hebrew midwives, of whom the name of one was Shiphrah and the name of the other Puah; and he said, "When you do the duties of a midwife for the Hebrew women, and see them on the birthstools, if it is a son, then you shall kill him; but if it is a daughter, then she shall live."
>
> Exodus 1:15–16

We also read in Scripture that Satan, through Herod, hoped to kill the infant Jesus by slaughtering all the male babies in the area who were two years old and under (see Matthew 2:16). Today, as noted earlier, we see an astronomical abortion rate and an all-time high of child abuse and exploitation. Many of the people we deal with in counseling and deliverance have experienced trauma before age two or at about age two. I am continually amazed and astounded at how many kids are abused.

Satan uses many means to attack children, even in the womb. His number one tactic obviously is abortion. If he cannot kill the child, he then attacks his or her soul through the means of rejection or fear. Oftentimes Satan will use the circumstances of a child being conceived out of wedlock, conceived at an inconvenient time or being otherwise unwanted to sow seeds of rejection.

A child's natural sense of hearing is developed while in the womb, long before it is born. It is my personal belief that a child's spirit, the "spirit man" part of his or her being, can hear at conception. It follows, then, that if the parents fight or the mother is a battered wife, the rejection and fear released in the atmosphere will also affect the child. A woman in a bad marriage has a 237 percent greater risk of bearing an emotionally damaged child than a woman in a loving marriage.[4] Babies born into families with bad relationships between the husband and wife are five times more fearful, jumpy or undersized, and they often respond negatively in other ways as they grow up.[5] It sticks with you!

On the other hand, positive words can affect a child before it is born as well. I remember hearing years ago, before the days of sonograms that reveal the growing child's sex, of parents who spoke to their baby every day while it was still in the womb. When the little boy was born, the father said, "Hi, Aaron!" Immediately, the baby swung his head around and smiled at his father.

The nurse said, "You've been talking to your baby."

To which the father replied, "Yes, and we named him or her Aaron or Erin so either way we had the name right." The baby knew his name and his father's voice.

A biblical example of this early cognition is found in this familiar passage:

> Now Mary arose in those days and went into the hill country with haste, to a city of Judah, and entered the house of Zacharias and greeted Elizabeth. And it happened, when Elizabeth heard the greeting of Mary, that the babe leaped in her womb; and Elizabeth was filled with the Holy Spirit. Then she spoke out with a loud voice and said, "Blessed are you among women, and blessed is the fruit of your womb! But why is this granted to me, that the mother of my Lord should come to me? For indeed, as soon as the voice of your greeting sounded in my ears, the babe leaped in my womb for joy."
>
> Luke 1:39–44

Wounding words and unhealthy family relationships are not the only factors that cause children to feel rejected from birth; even the threat of abortion brings harm to the baby. Babies can be born with a strong spirit of fear and rejection, often as a direct result of a mother who contemplated aborting her child. If the mother had an abortion previous to this baby, then the baby is often born with a spirit of death, due to death entering her mother's womb during the abortion.

After the child is born, the potential for harm and rejection certainly increases. A lot of babies who have fear in the womb do not want to come out and consequently have difficult deliveries. They have heard the violence, abuse and mess going on around them and have decided to stay in the womb. We can't really blame them, can we?

When the child is born, he or she might be the "wrong" sex (and the parents voice this). A child may be born with birth defects or learning disabilities, which give him or her a feeling of rejection or inferiority. A baby may not properly bond with the mother. Babies need to be held, cuddled, loved and generally made welcome. This is one reason why nursing is so important. Babies may be deprived of this special bonding due to medical emergencies or a mother who just does not choose to nurse or bond with her child. Adopted children often feel rejected as well, wondering why their real parents did not want them.

As children grow up, many are adversely affected by a large number of things. An absentee father (usually) or mother can hurt a growing child, giving him or her feelings of not being wanted or loved. Being compared to or placed in competition with siblings through statements like, "Why can't you be like your brother?" or "Your sister always gets good grades" can cause feelings of inferiority and low self-esteem. Physical, verbal or emotional abuse (screaming, yelling, degrading, constantly criticizing or controlling) will hurt the child as will sexual abuse, incest, molestation or rape. Young children around the ages of six to ten years old are the ones who seem to experience sexual abuse most often. Sadly, most women who have been sexually abused were abused by a family member or a close family friend.

Often kids take the blame for a divorce with the thought that *It's my fault Dad or Mom left* or they are made middlemen or mediators in marital problems. Alcoholism, drug abuse or sexual immorality displayed in the home affects children. Constant fighting, unjust discipline and shame also wound these kids. Being left alone because of a parent's work schedule or social activities add to a child's feelings of rejection. This is often the case in single-parent homes in which the parent works all day and then goes out at night because he or she is also hurt and looking for love.

Then when the children start school, they are often hurt by teachers or other students. Things such as being falsely accused of doing something or having a potty problem and being ridiculed for it allow shame and embarrassment to set in. We all know that kids can be cruel. If a child is not "just right," then others will surely pick on him or her. Being the last one chosen for a team or being called "four-eyes" or "ugly" or "fat" or "stupid" opens the door for rejection. And, of course, it does not stop there. Teens and adults suffer from broken relationships and, in today's promiscuous society, the sexual bonding and breaking that often goes with it. We can add emotional problems, sickness, job loss, physical challenges and even pain inflicted on those who are newly born again and come into the Body of Christ only to get hurt by the Church. The very ones who are supposed to accept them and love them unconditionally are the ones who turn around and reject them. God forbid that we should destroy these little ones, but, as the old saying goes, hurt people hurt people.

Also note that spirits of fear—including terror, trauma and nightmares—can come in from horror movies or from accidents like falling down the stairs, almost drowning in a pool or being in a car accident.

These are all real problems that cause real hurts that need real healing. Not everyone is wounded by every appearance of adversity, of course, and many who are wounded are able to find healing. But if the door of a person's heart has been opened by hurts or reactions to hurts, and if spirits have been able to place demonic hooks inside, then deliverance and inner healing are called for.

Victimization

We have seen numerous instances of victimization, but I want to talk about it in more depth for a moment. Doris Wagner calls it the "rotten ploy of victimization" in her book *How to Cast Out Demons*.[6] As pointed out earlier, the devil and his demons prey on the innocent and the weak, and they do *not* fight fair.

Recently I was praying and the Lord brought to my remembrance one of Gary Larsen's most memorable *Far Side®* comics. You may recall it. It depicted two deer (two bucks) standing upright, and one had his arm around the other's shoulder. He said to him, "Bummer of a birthmark, Hal." Hal had a large bull's-eye on his chest. Now that certainly is a bummer of a birthmark for a deer during hunting season! Well, the Lord spoke to me and said that we all have the very same birthmark.

In Isaiah 49:1 the prophet says: "Listen to me, you islands; hear this, you distant nations: Before I was born the LORD called me; from my birth he has made mention of my name" (NIV).

When God mentioned your name and mine, every host of heaven, as well as every demon of hell, heard it loud and clear. At that moment when our names were spoken, a target was placed on each of us by the enemy, and an assignment was placed against us. We see the results of it every day in counseling and deliverance.

Nowhere is it more evident than in ministry. All across America, men of God are falling into sin, most of which is sexual sin. A typical instance was the story in an Alabama newspaper about a young denominational youth pastor being sentenced to six years in jail for having sex with a fourteen-year-old girl in his youth group. The paper reported that prior to sentencing he apologized to the church, the community, his wife and his two small children.

Do you think he woke up one morning and said, "I think I will ruin my life today"? I don't think so. No, he let sin creep in slowly. I am sure he first lusted over that girl. Then he flirted with that girl. Then one thing led to another.

Years ago we had a powerful guest speaker at the school. God used him mightily. He challenged us as much as any speaker we have ever had. Yet within a matter of days he was arrested for making an obscene phone call. How can that be? How can you have a heart for God and for souls, yet be bound in perversion? It is because of hooks and strongholds! It is because of the assignments against us! Not very long after that incident, a pastor and his wife took in a seventeen-year-old girl, a foster child. No, the pastor did not fall; his wife fell into a lesbian affair and ran off with that seventeen-year-old girl. The pastor was so devastated that it rendered him totally ineffective. He eventually resigned his church and got a divorce. Are you getting the picture? It is a real war, with real bullets and with real casualties.

Tragedies and Transitions

Tragedies and transitions are other times when doors are opened in our lives to the demonic because of emotional wounding. During times of tragedy (death, divorce, severe illness, random acts of violence, disasters, accidents) Satan bombards us with depression. Then the spirits of doubt, worry, fear and defeat come into our lives.[7]

We start to believe the lies of the enemy that our lives are over, lies like, "I will never have a normal life" or "It is my fault that this or that took place."

Transitions are also wide open doors, particularly physical ones such as pregnancy, menopause and puberty. They make us vulnerable to attack by affecting our emotions, attitudes and actions. In other words, the physical changes in our bodies produce stress in our souls. During pregnancy many women inflict themselves with word curses, saying things like, "I'm fat"; "I'm ugly"; "I'll never look right again"; " No one will ever want me again." Menopause can cause feelings of being old, ugly and unwanted. This drives both men and women to look for affirmation, attention and affection, usually in all the wrong places, all of which can open doors to the enemy.

Jack Hayford says that more demonic strongholds enter people's lives during puberty than at any other time of life.[8] These doors are opened by exploration and experimentation in areas such as pornography, fondling, masturbation and intercourse, including homosexuality and lesbianism.

Pastor Sonny Jaynes of the pastoral care department at Brownsville Revival School of Ministry wrote the following points on homosexual behavior after 25 years of ministry, including work and counseling with homosexuals.

1. The doorway into this lifestyle usually begins in the early years before young adulthood or adolescence as a result of a father's rejection either by divorce or just plain neglect. There is usually an overprotective mother who is very controlling. Since there is no intimacy between the child and the father, the child begins to be confused about his true identity. Before the Industrial Revolution, homosexuality was rarely evident since young boys spent most of their daylight hours working on the farm with their fathers.

2. There may have been a sexual encounter during the early stages of puberty. This could happen in an innocent, exploratory way since a lot of children have had no instruction by the parents to prepare them for the changes they are to encounter. It could also be from something forced on them by someone older, perhaps even a close relative. Since there is no open communication with the parents, it is kept secret—this then leads to further confusion. This encounter could be easily mistaken for the love they are missing since it gives the child some form of gratification.

3. Sexual encounters in high school or college with members of the same sex are then easier to fall into since there has already been a previous sexual experience.

4. This leaves an open door for more confusion and
   allows the devil access into the life of the person involved, planting seeds of doubt as to sexual identity.
   Any attempt to rebuke will just result in further hard-
   ening of the person's heart.
5. As sexual contact continues, the person becomes more
   and more obsessed with sexual gratification. This
   leads to deeper and deeper bondage. The longer a
   person is involved in this lifestyle, the less chance
   there is of change.

Homosexuality is a lie that often comes in through emotional, verbal or sexual abuse. We are seeing an alarming
increase in the number of men who have been abused as
children who now struggle with homosexual thoughts or
tendencies. As homosexuals continue to come out of their
closets, more and more of them are trying to get in our
children's closets.

Inner Hurts and Outward Behavior

Feelings of deep inner hurt from any one of these areas
we have discussed generally manifest themselves in out-
ward behavior. Rebellion is the number one reaction to
rejection, hurts and abuse.[9] Rebellion is often accompanied
by anger, rage, violence, bitterness, hatred, jealousy, envy,
strife and extreme competition. Another major reaction
is a poor self-image, including feelings of inferiority, low
self-esteem, self-pity, sorrow and grief.

A constant feeling of low self-esteem will do several
things. First, it "paralyzes our potential."[10] If we are suffering from poor self-image we cannot do what we were
meant to do. Second, it steals our dreams and desires. We
think we are no good and cannot do anything. Third, it
ruins our relationships. "Satan uses your nagging sense of

inferiority and inadequacy to isolate you."[11] We fear reaching out to others or letting them know who we really are. Fourth, low self-esteem sabotages our Christian service. Teaching a class is difficult: "I can't get in front of people. I get too nervous." So is giving a testimony: "Oh, no way! I'm too shy." Knocking on doors and witnessing is impossible: "I would be scared to death!"

Some people choose to escape the reality of emotional pain by daydreaming, taking drugs, drinking alcohol or becoming addicted to television, computers or work. Some of us become defensive, argumentative and critical when we have been rejected. We may give way to perfectionism (always striving to please others, especially God). Other manifestations are distrust, doubt, worry, anxiety, stress and unbelief. Sometimes we try to protect ourselves by becoming self-righteous, arrogant, smug, self-centered, selfish, manipulative, controlling or possessive.[12]

Another way people deal with inner hurts is to make vows. We say things like, "No one's going to hurt me again"; "I'll never get married"; "I'll never have kids"; "Nobody is going to push me around again"; "I'll never let anyone else get close to me again"; "Nobody is going to control me again." We make vows to protect our emotions. Then we wonder why we are so rebellious or why we cannot or will not submit to our spouses, our bosses or our pastors. Men who have hurts usually turn to "machoism"; nothing is too tough for them to handle on their own. They bury the emotions and just live with the pain. Some women do this, too, but this is more often the "manly" way to handle it.

Another way we deal with hurts is to become angry and try to hurt others before we can be hurt. We may become defensive and argumentative. We try to convince others that we are right at all costs. We forget that when Jesus was falsely accused He never once defended Himself.

And finally, we sometimes resort to a subtle form of witchcraft in our hurt and pain. We attempt to influence our circumstances and their surroundings through manipulation and control.[13] We think that if everything is just right around us, then nothing or no one is going to hurt us; thus, we feel safe from any future hurts. *Webster's Dictionary* defines *manipulation* as "managing or influencing shrewdly or deviously, controlling or tampering with, by skilled use, for personal gain." That is a concise definition of witchcraft!

Any time we find ourselves dealing with unforgiveness, bitterness or resentment, we need to realize there is an open door for the experience that hurt us to continue hurting us. It gives the devil perfect opportunity to continue to poke his hooks into those festering sores. But that does not have to continue. Inner healing and deliverance can remove the hooks and close the doors to wounding from rejection or abandonment or abuse. Remember, deliverance is a lot more than casting out demons. It deals with people's hurts and wounds and all the junk they carry from the past. It sets them so free.

Part 3

Ministering Deliverance and Inner Healing

Ten

The Basis for Ministry

I highly recommend having a counseling, inner healing and deliverance ministry in every Bible school or local church. I say this mainly because of the great need, but also because a Spirit-filled church or school provides a safe environment in which to receive ministry. Most Christians do not have what I call a "bull" demon, a Legion if you will, but many Christians do struggle with oppressing or tormenting spirits. As a result they suffer with such things as rejection, fear, heaviness, jealousy, lust and perversion. They also deal with a lot of hurts, bad habits and wrong mind-sets. These people can often be ministered to by merely showing them the truth in the Word of God, and the truth will set them so free!

Biblical counseling is a lot more than having a Bible on your desk or quoting Scripture to someone. Biblical counseling is giving godly advice or counsel based purely on the Word of God. It is not giving opinions or personal thoughts or convictions; it is seeing what the Word of God says about a person's need or circumstance and sharing it with that individual. All counselors should heed the strong warning found in James 3:1: "Not many of you should presume to be teachers, my brothers, because you know that we who teach will be judged more strictly" (NIV).

Recently I was in the position of defending this ministry of deliverance. I asked the Lord to help me explain what we do. He gave me a visual of a pie graph.

The graph showed that 75 percent of what we do in a deliverance setting is to help individuals renew their minds, replacing the lies that they have believed with the truth. That truth sets them so free! Another 20 percent of what we do consists of inner healing, dealing with wounding from past hurts and abuses. Only about 5 percent of what we do is actually dealing with demons or the demonic, but of course that is the exciting part that everyone wants to talk about, even though it involves the least time. So we can see that up to 95 percent of the work of deliverance is really just counseling and ministry time with the individual.

Our Call to Help the Hurting

This may be why the Lord clearly spoke to me recently and said, *The Church needs ministers much more than it needs preachers.* There are countless Christians and unbelievers alike who are struggling with the pain and torment of past hurts and abuse, and, as a result, are experiencing constant guilt, shame and condemnation. Although the Church has had and still has the best preachers in the world, the Church is full of hurting and wounded people. I believe the Church's greatest need today is for men and women of God who will devote their time, energy and tears to those who are suffering from past hurts and abuses. The world is full of lost and dying people, but how can we reach them if we cannot even minister to our own brothers' and sisters' needs?

We are the Body of the Lord Jesus Christ, and Jesus wants us to be a whole, happy, healthy, sound and productive body, fit for the Master's use:

> Now a leper came to Him, imploring Him, kneeling down to Him and saying to Him, "If You are willing, You can make me clean." Then Jesus, moved with compassion, stretched out His hand and touched him, and said to him, "I am willing; be cleansed."
>
> Mark 1:40–41

Jesus is still willing. He did not come just to save us and give new birth to the "spirit man," but He came to heal our bodies and souls (minds, wills and emotions) as well. Jesus came to set the captives totally free.

We, the Church, are responsible as the Body of Christ to provide an atmosphere of *love, trust, transparency, unity* and *support* for all those who are hurting.[1] I believe the true power of God is love. Love is why God gave His only Son to die a horrible death for our sins. Love must be why He puts up with us. We, in turn, must also minister in love. We need to "above all things have fervent love for one another, for 'love will cover a multitude of sins'" (1 Peter 4:8).

Trust is as important as love. People need to know they can trust you with their innermost feelings and hurts, their wounds and disappointments, and their dirty laundry. We must be a people of integrity, people whom others feel comfortable with and safe to confide in. We should also be transparent and open with people—not to the point that they lose respect for us, but to the point that they know we are real people with real problems just like them, and we can indeed relate to their needs. Transparency does two things. First, it gives people hope. They see that you have overcome and are being used by God in spite of your flaws and shortcomings. Second, it keeps people from idolizing preachers, leaders and counselors. They need to keep their focus on Jesus and not on man.

Let me stress that point for a moment. People get attached to someone who has helped or is helping them. Watch for signs of dependency. Watch also that you do not become emotionally involved with the person you are ministering to. The devil would like nothing more than to pervert the compassion that God has given you and cause you to stumble and fall into sexual sin. Only God Himself knows how many men and women of God have fallen for that ploy of the devil.

We also need to be a unified Body of Christ. If you break a toe, your whole body knows it and your whole body feels it. Your whole body also compensates for it. It should be no different in the Body of Christ. When one person is hurting, we should all feel it, and we should all compensate for it. We must have compassion and love for one another just as Christ has for us.

We need to support one another till the very end. All too often, counselors and pastors get frustrated with people who seem to struggle continually in certain areas of their lives. This is understandable, but we have to remember Jesus taught us that the good shepherd would leave the 99 and seek after the lost one. We cannot give up on our brothers and sisters no matter how hopeless it looks, no matter how frustrating it gets. No matter how big a mess they are or they appear to be, we need to be there for them and to give them total, unconditional love and support. Remember, all it takes is one encounter with Jesus, and they can be made whole.

I believe one of the biggest disappointments in relation to the Church has been her failure to provide a healthy atmosphere of love, care and understanding. I dread to think of the number of hurting people who have backslidden or have been lost because we, the Body of Christ, have been too busy, too lazy or simply unwilling to go the extra mile with the hurting and wounded. People have come to us for help, but we have failed to do what we are called to do. There is a hurting world out there, but, even more tragic, there is a hurting and wounded Church out there. We are supposed to make a difference to these people. We are supposed to be a beacon of light and hope to them. We, the Church, are supposed to make the world jealous for what we have.

Let me ask you a question. When was the last time a neighbor followed you to church because he or she wanted what you had? The fruit of the Spirit is love, joy, peace, patience, kindness, goodness, faithfulness, gentleness and self-control (see Galatians 5:22–23). These things should be evident in our lives, visible to those around us. Before you minister to another, consider: How are you doing in this area of your life?

Guidelines for Ministry

I want to offer you now a few specifics to follow as you minister; in the next chapter we will discuss several cautions and safeguards.

Use a Good Questionnaire

A tremendously helpful tool for counseling, deliverance and inner healing is a good questionnaire. The questionnaire we developed at Righteous Acts Ministries, Inc., can be found in Appendix 1: Confidential Questionnaire. I also highly recommend the questionnaire found in Doris Wagner's book *How to Cast Out Demons*, which served as the basis for our own study. By using a good questionnaire you can avoid countless hours of digging, probing and searching for root causes of depression, eating disorders, suicidal thoughts and other torments that cause people to seek counseling and deliverance. In fact, after you review a completed questionnaire with people who have filled it out honestly, you will probably know them better than their own mother.

A questionnaire also reveals hidden areas that folks often find easier to write about than to talk about. When the facts are out in the open you will be much more effective in ministering to that person. Anything held in secret and in darkness is owned and controlled by the devil. If it is brought out into the light and exposed, his power can be destroyed. I liken it to a roll of film in a camera. If you open the back of the camera, the film is exposed to the light and destroyed.

The First Visit

I recommend giving the questionnaire to those seeking ministry on their initial visits. Do not have them fill it out at your office or place of ministry. Instead, instruct them to take it home, fill it out prayerfully and honestly, and bring it back on the next visit.

On the initial visit you should discuss unforgiveness issues. This is such a major issue, I am going to devote most of chapter 12 to it. For now let me say that neither deliverance nor inner healing sessions will be productive unless unforgiveness issues are dealt with effectively.

Thus, along with the questionnaire I assign other homework. I ask them to make a list of those who have hurt them. I tell them to get alone with God and ask Him to show them anyone and everyone who has ever hurt them in any way.

Here is a prayer that you can direct them to pray:

Heavenly Father, if there is any unforgiveness or bitterness in me, I ask You to expose it to the light right now. Show me the offense, run the scene in my mind so that I might forgive the person and repent of my sin and ask You to forgive me. Show me now. In Jesus' name I pray, amen.

After they complete the list, they are to start at the top and write each person a letter. They need to address the offense and then tell the person that in spite of the hurt, pain or unfairness, they choose to forgive the person from that day forward. They may or may not want to mail the letters. Regardless, this physical act of forgiveness has amazing spiritual consequences.

Next I direct them to pray about another area often associated with unforgiveness: judgments, vows and oaths. It is not at all unusual, for instance, for a person to say she hated her mom and swore never to be like her. Yet today she not only acts like her mother and does the very same things her mother did, but she even looks like her mother. People are always amazed at how God reveals these instances, played out in their minds like scenes from a movie. Tell them that as vows and judgments surface, they must repent and then renounce and break the words they spoke as well as any thoughts or deeds associated with the judgments.

Inner Healing Guidelines

As you help people obtain healing from the damage caused by inner hurts and wounds, you may need to encourage them to take further simple steps toward recovery.

First, as counseling progresses and problems come to light, they will need to face the issues squarely with ruthless honesty and God's grace. They need to confront those awful, hidden childhood memories no matter how deep the hurt goes. They must also acknowledge the memories to another person. Some problems, in fact, cannot be solved until they are confessed to others. James 5:16 says to confess our faults one to another so that we may be healed. Some people miss their inner healing because they fail to share their deep memories and pains with another person due to shame or a lack of courage.

Second, they must accept their own responsibility in the matter. Now they might say, "Hey! I was the victim! I was sinned against. I was innocent." That may be true, but what about their response to what happened? How did they handle it later in life? None of us is responsible for what happened to us as children, but once we are older and able to make our own choices, we also become accountable for our actions and the decisions we make regarding our situations. Healing will never come to those who blame everyone else and do not accept their own responsibility.

Third, they must ask themselves if they want to be healed. Some people do not want to be healed because then they will not have anyone to blame their problems on. Or they fear that they will not know how to act if they get healed. Or they fear that they will not know who they really are. Or they fear that they will lose a lot of attention. John 5:1–15 gives the account of the man at the pool of Bethesda. He had been lame for 38 years. When Jesus asked him if he wanted to be healed, the man wanted to chat: "Lord, no one will help me into the water." He was really having a pity party, and that is what a lot of us do also. It is an important question: Do I really want to be healed?

Fourth, at the appropriate time in ministry you will need to ask the Holy Spirit to reveal the real problem, the "root" problem. He can and will do it. He will run the video in their minds so that they can see even into the womb, crib or play-pen. Our Father in heaven wants us to be made whole.

Determining the Need for Deliverance

As your prayer time progresses, you might determine the problem to be a deliverance issue. If so, you will need to prepare the individual for the deliverance session, letting him or her know what to expect and what not to expect from deliverance.

One rule I use in determining whether or not to refer people to deliverance teams is if, regardless of what they do, they cannot seem to get relief from torment. These are people who are praying, reading the Word, active in praise and worship, seeking God, and who have gone through all the forgiveness issues, yet they are still unable to press through to victory.

If you cannot discover the root problem by talking with these people, counseling them or ministering in the area of inner healing, and if you hit a wall where they cannot receive healing in a particular area, then there is probably a demonic hindrance.

I do not recommend anyone for deliverance, however, who I feel has a weak Christian walk or who does not have the self-discipline it takes to walk it out. A good way to gauge people's ability to walk out deliverance is by how well they fight the battle before deliverance. Deliverance is not a quick fix. They need to be taught how to fight and take authority over the power of the enemy, and how to submit to God and resist the devil. If they are grounded enough to do this before deliverance, you can feel good about taking them through deliverance and breaking the strongholds that are hindering them.

Guidelines for Deliverance Sessions

Always begin each deliverance session by greeting everyone. Ask how everyone is doing. See if anyone is going through a rough time. Remember, you are doing spiritual warfare.

Open with prayer. Thank the Lord for the opportunity to minister to your sister or brother. Ask the Lord to come in power and set the person so free. Plead the blood of Jesus over each of you, and anoint the person with oil. I then like to bind all strongholds, and spirits of control, hiding and escape.

Have the person receiving ministry pray the deliverance prayer (see Appendix 2), the prayer regarding soul ties (see Appendix 3) and the prayers for breaking curses of death (see Appendix 4). If applicable, have the person pray to break any Vietnam curses (see Appendix 5). If the person has any connections with Freemasonry, you will need to break those curses. (One such prayer can be found on our RAM website at www.ramministry.org or the Jubilee Resources International website at http://www.jubilee.org.nz.)

Proceed to strongholds. In Appendix 6 you will find a comprehensive list. Depending on your workload, you will probably want to go through all of these. The entire process takes on average about four three-hour sessions. Or you may want to focus on the areas where you know problems exist. The Holy Spirit will guide you.

Have the person renounce the strongholds you are working on and the manifestations and fruits. After the individual has prayed, the team captain should call up each fruit listed and deal with it based on any manifestations and any prompting from the Holy Spirit. (The Holy Spirit will show you or others on your team how to pray; you need just to trust Him.) Inner healing is usually necessary when ministering in the strongholds of heaviness and fear, and sometimes in the area of haughtiness.

In closing the deliverance session be sure to bind all strongholds and tell them their only assignment is to go. Bind and gag all lying spirits. Close with prayer and thank the Lord for what He did in your sister's or brother's life.

Then pray blessings over the person. (See Appendix 7.)

Sometimes, when it takes several sessions for a person to obtain freedom through deliverance, you might need to counsel the individual in order to help him or her through some of the hard times. You will need to encourage him or her and be able to answer any questions that might arise during a session.

In large ministries the primary counselor is not always involved with the deliverance session; a separate team ministers deliverance. In this case, I do not recommend that the deliverance team also offer counseling. If more than one counselor is giving advice, it only gets confusing for the individual seeking help. Also, the primary counselor might not know everything that has been shared and what advice has been given by the deliverance team.

Follow-through

It is important for the ministry leader to follow up with the individual after the deliverance is complete. This is to make sure the person is walking in total freedom and also to help him or her recognize when the enemy tries to come back, because the enemy *will* try to come back. Appendix 8 gives an example of scriptural prayer to help in that new walk of freedom.

Let's turn now to a few safeguards for the deliverance minister.

Eleven

Cautions in the Ministry of Deliverance

A pastor friend of mine, Randy Worrell, once told me something profound. He said, "Common sense is not common to everyone." This is so true. What may be obvious to one person may not be obvious at all to another. I would like, therefore, to take the opportunity to share with you some precautions that should be taken when working in the ministry of deliverance.

First and foremost is the matter of integrity. I cannot stress enough to you the importance of confidentiality. Everything people see and everything they hear in a deliverance session *must* stay in that session. If word gets out that your team cannot be trusted with confidential information, the integrity of your ministry is destroyed and your ministry is over. This means that great care must be taken in the selection of team members. They will be exposed to very sensitive information that, if revealed, could be not only embarrassing but also very damaging to the person being ministered to.

Second, deliverance should never be done without a proper pastoral covering. The spirit realm is nothing to be dabbled in! Acts 19:13–16 gives the account of the seven sons of Sceva and their foolishness in attempting to perform a deliverance:

> Then some of the itinerant Jewish exorcists took it upon themselves to call the name of the Lord Jesus over those who had evil spirits, saying, "We exorcise you by the Jesus whom Paul preaches." Also there were seven sons of Sceva, a Jewish chief priest, who did so. And the evil spirit answered and said, "Jesus I know, and Paul I know; but who are you?" Then the man in whom the evil spirit was leaped on them, overpowered them, and prevailed against them, so that they fled out of that house naked and wounded.

The New International Version says that they fled "naked and bleeding"! I want you to know, regardless of how you translate it, that is a poor witness. It also shows us that without a right relationship with Jesus, we have no business ministering in the area of deliverance. In fact, it can be extremely dangerous.

Third, when dealing with demons, spirits or strongholds, do not become afraid of them or spooked by them. Philippians 4:6 says, "Be anxious for nothing," and that includes demons. "You are of God, little children, and have overcome them, because He who is in you is greater than he who is in the world" (1 John 4:4).

You must never, ever show fear, even if you feel it. Let me give you an illustration. In one deliverance session a couple of years ago, a young woman was praying prayers of repentance and renunciation that we start each session with. Suddenly, a growl started coming out from within her while she was reading. She continued to read, but as she did so the demon kept growling louder and louder and louder.

The team captain, who was sitting facing the woman, became visibly nervous. At the same time another woman standing behind the team captain started spinning like a top, grabbing her throat and choking. Then the team captain also started choking, grabbed her own throat and fell to the floor. I jumped up and commanded the demon to stop, and it did immediately. I took over and finished the session. The team captain quit the team. The other woman who was affected physically stayed with the ministry and is now one of my team leaders.

There were five team members in this particular session, but only two were affected by this spirit. I believe the two women who were affected probably showed some evidence of fear. When the demon was growling during the initial prayers, it amazed us all, but the spirit targeted them for attack in order to disrupt the session and delay his expulsion. Even if you are afraid, do not show it. If you do, you have already lost the battle.

Here is another incident. A young man that my wife and I both know told Janet of a dream he had had. In his dream, he had come in for a deliverance session and Janet had called up a particular spirit. That spirit manifested and left. Janet and I agreed to schedule an appointment with him to take him through deliverance, even though we were not aware of any reason that he should need deliverance.

On the day of the session, I felt as though the Lord was directing me to bring a "helper" with me. When we arrived, Janet asked why I had brought a helper. I told her God had told me to, and I was just being obedient. To make a long story short, we prayed about what he had seen in his dream, and the session soon got wild. At one point, he let out a fierce growl and lunged at me. This could have been an ideal opportunity for fear to manifest in me, my helper or my wife. Instead, I, too, yelled instinctively and lunged back at him, and we met in the middle and proceeded to fall to the floor. As quickly as it started, it ended. This big guy soon burst into tears and a generational spirit of anger, rage and violence that he had struggled with all his life broke in this young man's life. He is now married and a missionary to a foreign land. Thank You, Jesus!

Fourth, do not become fascinated by the demonic. That is a ploy of the devil to get your focus on him instead of on Jesus. It seems people are naturally drawn to the demonic and to evil; I suppose it has to do with our Adamic sinful nature. Whatever the reason, we need to be extremely careful. Look how Jesus addressed His disciples in Luke 10:17–20:

> Then the seventy returned with joy, saying, "Lord, even the demons are subject to us in Your name."
> And He said to them, "I saw Satan fall like lightning from heaven. Behold, I give you the authority to trample on serpents and scorpions, and over all the power of the enemy, and nothing shall by any means hurt you. Nevertheless do not rejoice in this, that the spirits are subject to you, but rather rejoice because your names are written in heaven."

When the disciples returned all excited because they could cast out demons, Jesus was not impressed. In essence He said to them, "Big deal; I saw Satan himself cast down from heaven like a bolt of lightning. Demons are nothing. Rejoice because you are saved, not because demons obey you." Jesus was saying that salvation is the greatest miracle of all. Jesus was also cautioning His disciples to keep their perspective clear in this area of deliverance. I recommend that we, too, heed His warning and do the very same. Satan would like nothing more than to get our focus off of Jesus and onto him.

Fifth, always work in teams. Never work alone, and especially never work alone with a member of the opposite sex. The devil will do everything in his power to stop this ministry, everything from temptation to false allegations. If you give him an inch, he will surely take a mile. Even Jesus sent His disciples out in pairs: "After these things the Lord appointed seventy others also, and sent them two by two before His face into every city and place where He Himself was about to go" (Luke 10:1).

I prefer to work with a team of five. The ideal team has at least three women and two men. If you are dealing with a woman, she will be comforted by the presence of three other women. That way, too, if you are working with a man you will have at least two men to assist you if he manifests with unnatural or supernatural strength. (Please note: Women will manifest unnatural strength as well.)

The following is a diagram of how I prefer to set up a deliverance session:

wall
‡◊‡
X
OOO

Seat the person you are ministering to (◊) with his or her back against the wall and a team member of the same sex (‡) on each side of him or her.

These members can quickly restrain the person you are working with, and they can exhort the person during the session by whispering in his or her ears things like, "It's the blood, the blood of Jesus" or "It's the love of God" or "It's the Father's love." These things drive the evil spirits nuts, and these truths set the captive free. How free? You guessed it! *So free!* The team leader (X) is seated directly in front of the person being ministered to. The three team members (O) behind the team leader can pray in tongues, read Scriptures and assist in any other way needed during the session. As I have mentioned, I often have one of the team members record all that is said and everything that takes place in the session. As liability concerns grow, it may be wise to have a record of what transpires in the sessions.

I often have a person behind the team leader read specific Scriptures as well while I am commanding the spirit to leave. When dealing with a Jezebel spirit, for instance, I direct a team member to read 2 Kings 9:30–37:

> Then Jehu went to Jezreel. When Jezebel heard about it, she painted her eyes, arranged her hair and looked out of a window. As Jehu entered the gate, she asked, "Have you come in peace, Zimri, you murderer of your master?"
>
> He looked up at the window and called out, "Who is on my side? Who?" Two or three eunuchs looked down at him. "Throw her down!" Jehu said. So they threw her down, and some of her blood spattered the wall and the horses as they trampled her underfoot.
>
> Jehu went in and ate and drank. "Take care of that cursed woman," he said, "and bury her, for she was a king's daughter." But when they went out to bury her, they found nothing except her skull, her feet and her hands. They went back and told Jehu, who said, "This is the word of the LORD that he spoke through his servant Elijah the Tishbite: On the plot of ground at Jezreel dogs will devour Jezebel's flesh. Jezebel's body will be like refuse on the ground in the plot at Jezreel, so that no one will be able to say, 'This is Jezebel.'"
>
> NIV

This Scripture, read over and over, will drive the Jezebel spirit nuts. Another thing that will disrupt the Jezebel spirit and ultimately drive it out is to speak blessings over the person.

Whenever we are dealing with a spirit of Antichrist, I like to have a team member read Daniel 7:9–12:

"As I looked, thrones were set in place, and the Ancient of Days took his seat. His clothing was as white as snow; the hair of his head was white like wool. His throne was flaming with fire, and its wheels were all ablaze. A river of fire was flowing, coming out from before him. Thousands upon thousands attended him; ten thousand times ten thousand stood before him. The court was seated, and the books were opened.

"Then I continued to watch because of the boastful words the horn was speaking. I kept looking until the beast was slain and its body destroyed and thrown into the blazing fire. (The other beasts had been stripped of their authority, but were allowed to live for a period of time.)"

NIV

The Word of God is indeed sharper than any two-edged sword. Using the Word in this way is like a scalpel surgically cutting hell out of people's lives. It is an awesome thing to see!

This arrangement and use of team members has proven to be highly effective in multiplied hundreds of deliverance sessions.

Sixth, men need to be extremely sensitive regarding touching women. Most women we deal with in deliverance sessions (as many as nine out of ten) have been sexually molested or in some other way been physically abused, most often by men. Great care must be taken so we do not further inflict wounds on our sisters.

Men should never touch any part of a woman's body in a session except her arms, hands, shoulders, head or back. Men should *never* put their hands on a woman's heart (chest) or stomach area. One of the women on the team can do this if the team leader deems it necessary and gains the individual's permission. Hugs can be a wonderfully effective part of ministry, but never hug a woman, or a man for that matter, without first asking her (or his) permission. Only do so with other team members present.

Seventh, I have given several examples of demons being unwilling to leave and the fights that ensued. I want you to understand the possibility for attack is real and often comes from every direction—not just physical attacks in the deliverance setting. There may be attacks on your thought life, your family, your marriage, your finances, even your vehicles. Now I am certainly not trying to discourage anyone from this ministry because the need is so great, but I want team leaders and members to know the amount and severity of the attacks that often come so you can be prepared physically, mentally, emotionally and, of course, spiritually. You need to be "prayed up" and "fasted up."

Likewise, be prepared to hear anything and everything. In sessions you will hear people's personal experiences that will appall you and at times even sicken you. You will hear of every kind of abuse from bestiality and incest to rape and murder. You may hear of abuses that happened to your own children or other family members. You might even hear things that you did to others prior to your salvation. When these things come up, the devil will bombard you with flashbacks of your past hurts, pains and abuses. He may bombard you with guilt, shame or condemnation. He will do anything and everything he can to render you ineffective. You will often leave sessions feeling slimed and dirty.

It must be noted, therefore, that this ministry is not for everyone. Some people are much more sensitive than others and will not be able to withstand the painful information or the attacks. If you are the team leader, you have a responsibility to keep an eye on your team. The enemy will try to isolate your members and pick them off, one by one. I have had team members break down, only to find out they had been under severe attack for weeks or even months. Be alert.

Finally, be aware that deliverance is not the solution for everything. It is not the answer to every need or every problem. Remember, there is not a demon behind every bush. Know that a lot of people are looking for a quick fix. We live in a world with a microwave mentality. We all want it our way, and we want it right now. Many people want to substitute deliverance for discipline. You cannot cast out "self," and you cannot cast out temptation; nor can you cast out bad habits, trials or tribulations.

Deliverance is not a game where someone is set free from bondage only to return to the junk of his past, open more doors and then seek deliverance again. I have ministered to people who have done this very thing and found the promise in Matthew 12:45 to be true: "The last state of that man is worse than the first." Actually, it was much worse. I would guess seven times worse.

Twelve

Why People Do Not Get Free

God desires for all His children to be free. Sadly, though, not everyone experiences freedom. There are several reasons people do not get free.

I believe many people do not get free because they do not repent of their sins. True repentance is a lot more than godly sorrow. True repentance is a change of heart and a change of attitude. It also is a change of direction. It is turning from sin and going the other way.

Another reason is because people are consumed with doubt and have unbelief. They do not believe that God really loves them or cares about them. They believe God's promises are for everyone else but them. They do not believe they can be free, and due to their unbelief they will not experience freedom.

Also, things like MPD and programming can stand in the way of freedom. SRA victims often have the mentality that they will always be victims, that they will never be free.

I once stated in a Cleansing Stream class I was leading, "Most of you will receive major freedom at the upcoming retreat."

Afterward a woman came up to me and told me she knew she would never get free, that they (her abusers) would come and get her and reprogram her. I suggested she move to another area, but she assured me they would just come after her. She believed she belonged to Satan and he would send someone after her. She was filled with unbelief!

People also fail to get free because they fail to break with the occult. Some people who have been involved in witchcraft and the occult do not want to lose their powers.

I mentioned earlier the importance of helping the person forgive everyone who has hurt him or her. Failure to forgive is a major reason why people do not experience complete freedom. Let us look at how important forgiveness really is.

The devil attacks in many ways. He attacks individually and corporately. He attacks health and finances. He attacks spouses and children. He tempts people with lusts and evil of every kind. Not only does he attack physically, but he also attacks the soulish realm. A person's mind, will and emotions become a battlefield of impure thoughts, vain imaginations, arguments, mental conflicts and confusion.

If Satan cannot cause someone to stumble in any other way, he will get a brother or sister to offend that person. When the offense occurs it has the potential to create hurt, anger, wrath, outrage, jealousy, resentment, strife, contention, bitterness, hatred, envy and even murderous thoughts. You will recall that Cain envied Abel's sacrifice and then killed him (see Genesis 4:3–8). Pilate knew that the Pharisees envied Jesus (see Mark 15:10).

People who are offended will manifest with anything from insults and sarcasm to outbursts of wrath and violence. These offenses cause division, separation, broken relationships and betrayal. Sadly, many people backslide over offenses, hurts and other things some carnal person did or said to them.

A person sets himself up for offense by expecting certain things from others. As T. D. Jakes is noted for saying, "You'll never be disappointed by what you don't expect!" As he explains, everyone has a level of expectation from parents, spouses, children, bosses, friends, pastors, co-workers, leaders, even congregations. The greater the expectations, the greater the potential for disappointment and the greater the offense.

I worked my way through Bible school doing pest control work; I believe God was preparing me for deliverance ministry. I had a particular customer in Alabama. One day when I went to service her home, I met her and her daughter coming out of the front door. She said they were on their way to go to "Uncle Rob's cremation."

When she told me that, I said, "Well, I sure hope Uncle Rob knew Jesus." She proceeded to tell me Uncle Rob was the most godly, sweetest man you could have ever known. He would do anything for you. He would give you the shirt off his back. If you needed help, he would drop what he was doing and come help you any time day or night.

But (and, yes, *but* here means disregard everything she had just said) several years before he had gotten very sick and was hospitalized. No one from the church came to visit him—not even the pastor or any of the elders. Uncle Rob took such offense that when he recuperated, he actually changed his will and decided to be cremated so that no pastor could speak over him and bury him. He never went back to church. Uncle Rob died suddenly of a massive heart attack. Personally I question Uncle Rob's final destination. He never got over that offense.

Uncle Rob did not understand that when we become born again, we become Christians. As Christians we have no rights. We have no rights that need to be protected. John Bevere explains it this way: We need to be dead men and women.[1] First Corinthians 6:7 says, "Why do you not rather accept wrong? Why do you not rather let yourselves be cheated?" The answer is because we are not dead yet! You can go up to a man in a casket, say or do anything to him, and it will not offend him. Why? Because he is dead! Likewise, we should not allow ourselves to be offended by others, no matter how hard it is. If we are truly dead in Christ, we cannot be offended.

Proverbs 18:19 states: "A brother offended is harder to win than a strong city, and contentions are like the bars of a castle." If you are dealing in ministry with someone who has been hurt, he or she has likely put up walls around his or her emotions in order not to be hurt again. In some cases it may be more like a castle or a strong city (a stronghold). What was created to protect him or her, ends up being a prison. Second Corinthians 10:4–5 speaks of this:

> For the weapons of our warfare are not carnal but mighty in God for pulling down strongholds, casting down arguments and every high thing that exalts itself against the knowledge of God, bringing every thought into captivity to the obedience of Christ.

You see, the devil inhabits these places in the person's emotions, these strongholds. He is warring against that person's soul. He is warring against that person's knowledge of God and against his or her knowing God.

Offended people often twist the Word of God to defend themselves or to back their positions.[2] God's Word without love can actually be a destructive force. People can get puffed up with pride and legalism. Look at the Pharisees, the religious leaders of two thousand years ago. They knew the Word. They knew the Scriptures. They also put the Son of God to death. God calls us to rightly divide the Word, and we can only do that with love. Matthew 5:44 quotes these words of Jesus: "But I say to you, love your enemies, bless those who curse you, do good to those who hate you, and pray for those who spitefully use you and persecute you." Bless and do not curse; advance the Kingdom of God. God does not tell us to get even or hold a grudge or stay mad at our enemies. Jesus had more reason to take offense than anyone else in history. He left His place, His home in glory, and was born onto this earth. He spent 33 years in this sinful, dirty world and He remained sinless. He did signs and wonders, healed the sick, raised the dead, cast out demons and showed great compassion for the poor and needy. He did more good than anybody, yet He was falsely accused and arrested. He was beaten, whipped and spat upon. His beard was plucked out. He was stripped naked and nailed to a cross. He was publicly humiliated and tortured to death. Jesus had reason to be offended! But He took no offense. He did no wrong, and He did not sin.

> For to this you were called, because Christ also suffered for us, leaving us an example, that you should follow His steps:
> "Who committed no sin, nor was deceit found in His mouth";
> who, when He was reviled, did not revile in return; when He suffered, He did not threaten, but committed Himself to Him who judges righteously.
>
> 1 Peter 2:21–23

Not only did Jesus not sin, but He also asked God to forgive those who wronged Him: "Father, forgive them, for they do not know what they do" (Luke 23:34). When the disciples asked Jesus how they should pray, He directed them to say: "Forgive us our debts, as we forgive our debtors" (Matthew 6:12). Jesus went on to teach them: "For if you forgive men their trespasses, your heavenly Father will also forgive you. But if you do not forgive men their trespasses, neither will your Father forgive your trespasses" (verses 14–15).

Satan knows this Scripture; he knows that unforgiveness is just as much a sin as adultery, fornication, pornography or lying. He also knows that this, just like any other sin, opens the door and gives him a legal right to torment you and me and any person seeking counseling help. Offense and the unforgiveness that follows are among Satan's most powerful weapons against the Church.

Jesus gave us this parable:

"Therefore the kingdom of heaven is like a certain king who wanted to settle accounts with his servants. And when he had begun to settle accounts, one was brought to him who owed him ten thousand talents. But as he was not able to pay, his master commanded that he be sold, with his wife and children and all that he had, and that payment be made. The servant therefore fell down before him, saying, 'Master, have patience with me, and I will pay you all.' Then the master of that servant was moved with compassion, released him, and forgave him the debt.

"But that servant went out and found one of his fellow servants who owed him a hundred denarii; and he laid hands on him and took him by the throat, saying, 'Pay me what you owe!' So his fellow servant fell down at his feet and begged him, saying, 'Have patience with me, and I will pay you all.' And he would not, but went and threw him into prison till he should pay the debt. So when his fellow servants saw what had been done, they were very grieved, and came and told their master all that had been done. Then his master, after he had called him, said to him, 'You wicked servant! I forgave you all that debt because you begged me. Should you not also have had compassion on your fellow servant, just as I had pity on you?' And his master was angry, and delivered him to the torturers until he should pay all that was due to him.

"So My heavenly Father also will do to you if each of you, from his heart, does not forgive his brother his trespasses."

Matthew 18:23–35

As we look at this parable, we see that this man owed a great debt of 10,000 talents. One talent was the equivalent of 75 pounds of gold or silver, the common coinage of that day. So he owed 750,000 pounds of either gold or silver. That is 375 tons! Gold at $400 an ounce would be about $4.8 billion. Are you getting the picture? It was a debt he could not pay. This servant was forgiven much.

This same man, however, who was forgiven so much went out and found a fellow servant—not a heathen or an unbeliever, but a fellow brother in Christ. This fellow servant owed him 100 denarii. A denarii was a day's wage back then for a laborer. So figure $6 an hour times an eight-hour day is $48, times 100, and that equals a debt of $4,800. That is a fair amount of money, but it is a far cry from the millions or billions that the first servant was forgiven.

You may find that some people will consider this behavior of the first servant to be appalling, yet those individuals must ask themselves: Am I doing the same thing with a wife or husband, a mom or dad, a brother or sister, a used-to-be best friend, a boss, a pastor? Am I holding someone else to a debt—great or small—but expecting God to forgive my own sins? Am I accepting His forgiveness but not forgiving others? Do I hope God will punish others for what they have done?

Are you and I guilty of this as well?

This man's fellow servants were grieved and reported to their master what the servant had done. We can be sure that our sins will always find us out. Even if no one ever finds out, God always knows.

When he heard about the great injustice that had been done, the master was angry and delivered the unforgiving servant over to the torturers (tormentors) until he paid all that he owed. We know that it was impossible for this man to repay that debt. This man actually lost his salvation. He was saved, his debt had been forgiven, but he lost it. I wonder how many people reading this book or sitting in our churches are hell-bound because of unforgiveness.

This is the only known parable for which Jesus gave an unsolicited explanation to His disciples. He wanted the importance of forgiveness to be crystal clear, both then and now. Hurts are real; pain is real. No one questions that. Yet God speaks continually throughout Scripture about this issue of forgiveness. I believe the reason is that God knows we are going to hurt each other, and this gives an open door to the devil. God wants us to have love and compassion for one another. He longs for us to forgive each other just as in Christ, He forgave us (see Ephesians 4:25–32) so that we may be one in Him and show the love of Jesus to the world.

God's plan is not for His people to be turned over to the tormentors. Jesus said that the master delivered the servant to the torturers. This word *delivered* means "allowed" him to be tortured, but was not his will. He turned him over reluctantly. God's will is for His people to have joy and freedom in life and to spend eternity with Him in glory, but the Word says that everyone will reap what he sows. Pain and hardness from unforgiveness in a heart will bring only pain and hardness to that person's life. Doctors have even attributed some cancers and arthritis to unforgiveness.[3] As ministers of inner healing and deliverance, we must help others root out the unforgiveness that would allow these and other tormentors into their lives. And we must make sure that unforgiveness is not allowed to grow in our lives as well.

Jesus often refers to the heart as soil. When the Word of God takes root in a heart, it grows and produces the fruit of righteousness. But when a person plants unforgiveness, a root of bitterness will spring up. Francis Frangipane defines *bitterness* as "unfulfilled revenge." It is produced when revenge is not satisfied to the degree the person thinks it should be. Bitterness produces poison. Peter said to Simon the sorcerer: "For I see that you are poisoned by bitterness and bound by iniquity" (Acts 8:23). The writer of Hebrews tells us: "Pursue peace with all people, and holiness, without which no one will see the Lord: looking carefully lest anyone fall short of the grace of God; lest any root of bitterness springing up cause trouble, and by this many become defiled" (Hebrews 12:14–15).

I liken bitterness to weeds in a garden. I had a garden once, and I had a constant battle with this little two-leaf weed. The roots of this weed were about a quarter of an inch thick and four to five inches long. With or without rain the weeds flourished because their roots went so deep. At one point we were gone from home for several weeks and the garden went unattended. By the time we returned, the weeds had actually started choking out the vegetable plants.

That is exactly what bitterness will do. It will choke and poison any heart in which it is allowed to grow. It will poison thoughts, attitudes and eventually actions. Scripture is clear about bitterness and forgiveness: "Let all bitterness, wrath, anger, clamor, and evil speaking be put away from you, with all malice. And be kind to one another, tenderhearted, forgiving one another, even as God in Christ forgave you" (Ephesians 4:31–32).

You and I can set the example for those who are being choked by this root of unforgiveness and bitterness. We can choose to forgive. We can decide right now to be people of forgiveness. If He reveals any person or persons you need to forgive, do so now. We have to do it, whether our emotions like it or not. We have to understand that we will never be exempt from offense, rejection or hurts. Jesus said, "If they hate me, they will hate you," and "If they reject me, they will reject you." So get used to it. Expect it. And share this with others who need desperately to be set free.

Forgiveness is not a choice on our part. Peter wondered about this: "'Lord, how often shall my brother sin against me, and I forgive him? Up to seven times?' Jesus said to him, 'I do not say to you, up to seven times, but up to seventy times seven'" (Matthew 18:21–22). We have absolutely no right to hold anyone in unforgiveness. God will not tolerate our doing so. What a tragedy to be like Uncle Rob! For him to be such a good person, and still go to hell and spend eternity with the absolute worst of the world—Adolf Hitler, Jack the Ripper and the like. That is not what God wants for any of us. Why does it happen? Because of unforgiveness.

A lot of Christians will forgive those who hurt them, but they cannot seem to forgive themselves for what they have done to themselves or others or Jesus. They let guilt, shame and condemnation come in. Then they allow self-hate to take over. They will not forgive themselves for things that God has already forgotten and thrown into His sea of forgetfulness. But remember that Jesus said, "If you have anything against *anyone*, forgive him, that your Father in heaven may also forgive you your trespasses. But if you do not forgive, neither will your Father in heaven forgive your trespasses" (Mark 11:25–26, emphasis added).

Does any person have the right not to forgive himself if Jesus has forgiven him? No. And this goes also for those who blame God Himself for their pain and refuse to let Him soften the soil of their hearts with forgiveness. Forgiveness is a spiritual matter done out of obedience, obedience to the will of God and to the Word of God. It is not an emotional feel-good kind of thing; it is a choice. There is a dimension of freedom that will never happen in a person's life until he or she chooses to be a forgiving person. Without forgiveness, however, there will be *no* healing, period.

Holding someone in unforgiveness is like being connected to that person by an invisible chain. If you are bound to a person, he or she can hurt you the rest of your life—every time the memory of the hurt is replayed in your mind. Satan knows exactly what memory to stir up. He will use it in order to make you feel hopeless, worthless and defeated. Every time the scene plays, you will hurt all over again. But once you forgive that person who hurt you, God can and will go in and heal that hurt and break that chain forever.

Wholeness of body, soul and spirit has always been God's desire for His people. As our society and the world continue to deteriorate socially and morally, we will see more and more hurting and wounded people coming into our churches, needing forgiveness and needing to forgive. They will also be seeking truth and looking for answers to life's problems. It is such an honor and privilege to see what God can and will do with willing servants. It is truly a miracle to watch Him set people not just free, but so free!

In the next chapter you will read actual testimonies of changed lives as the result of the ministry described within these pages. I pray they will not only encourage you but also motivate you to deal with any areas of bondage you still struggle with in your own life and to help others get so free.

Thirteen

Testimonies of Deliverance

Here to encourage you are several testimonies from men and women who have found freedom through deliverance and inner healing ministry. Each person here and hundreds of others like them are witness to the love and power of Jesus Christ to break the chains of bondage and bring us into His marvelous light.

Early Bondage to Fear

Growing up with fear and control in my life seemed normal to me. But as I grew up in the Lord, they began to torment me and seemed to hold me back from the deep intimacy I longed for with the Lord.

After attending a Cleansing Stream Retreat at the end of my first semester at Brownsville Revival School of Ministry (BRSM), all of hell seemed to attack me physically and mentally. During a school chapel, I began to feel intense pressure on my chest and could hardly breathe. It really scared me.

After this, I set up an appointment with a deliverance team. The attacks grew more and more intense as it got closer to the time of the appointment. After my initial meeting, I was able to realize how my giving in to the enemy's tactics was dangerous for me; I was only helping him win.

Through the deliverance process, things from my past surfaced. Molestation in my family and a family tree of witchcraft began to be exposed. I had not realized how the sins of my parents and grandparents could so infiltrate my life and allow the enemy to influence the way I thought and acted.

Through the deliverance ministry at BRSM, God has shown me how I had allowed the enemy at a very early age to place bondages on me. Some bondages, I believe, came in as far back as conception (over which I had no control).

One thing I really have to say is how compassionate and loving the people were who ministered to me during the deliverance sessions. I was really nervous about going, but once I got there, I felt peace and the hand of God controlling everything. Demonic strongholds were broken, and God set me totally free from the bondages that had held me for so long. Physical pain actually left my body, but, most importantly, the peace of God flooded my soul. God is my *victor*! The difference in me was incredible after the deliverance.

I have to say my life has been totally transformed.

Uncontrollable Anger

I went through deliverance because I was very angry and frustrated in my marriage and all other relationships. I could not control my anger. I was very depressed, and I did not know why. I was a very angry mom and sometimes abusive. I was out of control. It's not that I didn't try to get help: I did, but nobody knew what to do. I believe that there could be a lot of marriages saved through deliverance ministry, and there would not be so many casualties in the Body of Christ.

The first thing I did was write letters to everybody who had hurt me, past and present. In the letters I confronted them with the truth and then forgave them. The Lord helped me remember everybody I needed to forgive. Before deliverance I was plagued with really bad memories every day. It was as though they haunted me: memories from a really bad childhood of rape and incest, etc. Since deliverance, those memories have no effect or power over me. I don't even think of those things anymore. And when I talk to the people who hurt me, I don't feel the pain from what they did. I really forgave them.

When we dealt with the spirit of anger, I got very angry in the session. I punched pillows and almost knocked Bill Sudduth over in his chair. I got it out and was delivered. I am so free! That's not just a cliché. My husband noticed my eyes were a lighter brown. When Bill saw me next he noticed the same thing. The greater evidence was in my actions. My relationships with my family changed so much. I did not know it could be so good.

Before deliverance I was having really bad dizzy spells; the dizzy spells would make me so sick. Sometimes I would have one while driving and almost wreck. In one of the deliverance sessions, I had one after the other. I almost threw up, it was so bad. I was delivered of something that day and have never had one since.

I was afraid I would go back to my old ways, but I didn't. It is a daily process of walking it out. It is very exciting because I am functioning as a normal child of God through His strength. I can love my family now, and my God. I can also minister to other people now. They spoke the truth to me, I received it and it set me free. I think a better name for this ministry is "So Free," because I am so free.

I would like to include here my daughter's testimony:

"Before my family was saved, my mom was always mad, weird and emotional. But when we came to Brownsville Assembly of God Church and my mom took deliverance, I could see a great change in her. She was always smiling, singing and buying things for me. And not only did she change, but the whole family changed! Now we have family time a lot, we go to church almost every day and we got rid of our TV. I have seen a great change in her life and I'm proud of her."

Out of the Tomb

The Holy Spirit brought the passage in John 11:38–44 about Jesus raising Lazarus to my mind several weeks ago. I began to look back over the past seven months and think about how much God has done in my life and the freedom and healing He has given me. Overwhelmed with His love and goodness, I began to see this passage as a personal summary of the road I have traveled with Jesus during these months.

Before ministry, I reeked of "death." I remember so many times, so many prayers prayed over me . . . speaking life back into me. I had been in my tomb for many years, but the ministry team listened to Jesus' command and began to "take away the stone." As the Holy Spirit walked me through my first inner healing session, they helped me and interceded for me. That first session was the first time I had ever felt Jesus' love for me. That was when Jesus, deeply moved, came to my tomb and called me out of my state of death.

Though I came out of the tomb, I was still wrapped in grave clothes. In verse 44, Jesus said to the people, "Take off the grave clothes and let him go." Jesus raised Lazarus from the dead but He wanted "them" to take off the grave clothes and release him. Once again, the team became "them" and responded to Jesus' request. Through the counseling, prayers and love, piece by piece, my soul and spirit were unwrapped. Then the deliverance team helped clean me up.

All honor and praise for my freedom and healing belong to Jesus. And I am so thankful and appreciative for the role the ministry teams have had in this "journey" of mine. Whether they realize it or not, they have poured so much into me—so many nuggets of truth that I will hold onto.

Turning Up the Heat

I knew there were areas of my life that I wanted God to take care of. I didn't know how or when, but I was determined God was going to change these areas in my life. God led me to seek deliverance. It was a very difficult time for me. The Lord started uprooting things from my past, including molestation as a child and perversion growing up, as well as the fear, anger and hatred of men that were results of these past hurts and abuses. When I was finished, I was so free! The Lord broke the strongholds off my mind. My mind was completely renewed. Even people back home say that I am a different person from when I left to go to school. Being in the midst of revival fire, God has turned up the heat in my life. He has burned away the dross and set me free. I can now be the woman of God He has called me to be.

Freedom from "Secret Sin"

When I was around the age of seven, I was introduced to masturbation. I had no idea really what that was. Well, that opened a door in my life for the devil to mess with my mind. Not only did I struggle with my thought life, but fear also had a major hold on me. During the day I would be fine; nothing ever bothered me at all. But as soon as I shut my eyes to sleep, either sexual thoughts or fear would come into my mind. It was so bad that I could not sleep, and during the night I would feel pressure on my chest and heart and almost could not breathe. A voice would tell me I was going to die.

I did not tell anyone about my struggles because I felt ashamed and dirty and very guilty for my "secret sin." I kept all my emotions, questions, situations and guilt bottled up inside of me. I was afraid that anyone who found out who I really was inside would not like me. When I came to Brownsville Revival School of Ministry, I heard about deliverance. I knew I needed to be set free and healed. When I went through deliverance I would get uncomfortable and want to leave, but I stayed, and Jesus set me free from fear, control and perversion! Since my deliverance, I have again been attacked in my thoughts, but I now know who I am in Christ. The devil does not want us as Christians to know who we are in Christ because when we realize the power of Jesus Christ, we realize that same power is in us. His strength is in us. Jesus set me free! So free! He taught me how to fight and say no. Praise the Lord for the freedom He has given me and the peaceful sleep He has blessed me with.

He Was There All Along

God has done an absolute miracle in my life. When I first came to BRSM, I wanted to serve Jesus with all my heart. The problem was that I was still mentally bound by my past. God had saved me from a life of homosexuality, alcohol, occult practices and suicide. I longed to be free from perverse thoughts.

After being so bombarded with demonic attack, I went to speak to pastoral care and was referred to the deliverance team (while still counseling me). During the sessions, the Lord showed me that He had been there all along. I had been a victim of molestation at the hands of a female babysitter, and later a priest. The excuse for rejecting God was rooted in this. I learned that Jesus loved me and had never wanted that to happen. It became real to me that I had always wanted to be the victim, while making God out to be the "bad guy."

There was one session where the Lord revealed the root of homosexuality in my life. When I was a child I was surrounded by a group of other kids who were laughing at me. A girl I liked proclaimed loudly how ugly I was. In the spirit world the Lord showed me how a demon was whispering into her ear. Jesus also showed me how He was there all along, crying and praying for me (along with many angels). At the age of eight I told myself, *I give up. I'll never have a wife. Girls don't like me.* From that point on I allowed homosexuality and bitterness toward women to root. With this exposed, I repented and renounced that word curse. The Lord cast out the lying spirit. To this day I am free from homosexuality, rejection, lying, fear, perversion, bondage, anger and jealousy. Jesus cut those strongholds down at the root. Hallelujah!

(Note: This brother is now living in the Midwest with his new wife.)

Appendix 1

Confidential Questionnaire

Name		Date
Address		
Phone	**Spiritual Counselor**	
Age	**Birthday**	
Marital Status ☐ Single ☐ Married ☐ Divorced ☐ Remarried ☐ Widowed		

General Information

1. What is your church background? Include denomination(s) and/or church experience.

2. When did you accept Jesus Christ into your life? Briefly describe your conversion experience.

3. Was your life really changed? ☐ Yes ☐ No
    If yes, how?

4. Have you been baptized since your conversion?
    ☐ Yes ☐ No
    If yes, when?

5. Do you have assurance of salvation? ☐ Yes ☐ No
    If no, please explain.

6. Have you been filled with the Holy Spirit? ☐ Yes ☐ No
    If yes, when, and what evidence have you seen?

7. Describe the content and frequency of your personal devotional and prayer time.

8. Where were you born (city, state, nation)?

9. Have you lived in other countries? ☐ Yes ☐ No
    If yes, which ones?

10. Have you traveled to other countries? ☐ Yes ☐ No
    If yes, which ones?

Family Background and Relationships

11. Where was your father born (city, state, nation)?

12. Where was your mother born (city, state, nation)?

13. Were you a planned child?
    ☐ Yes ☐ No ☐ Don't know

14. Were you the "right" sex? ☐ Yes ☐ No ☐ Don't know

15. Were you conceived out of wedlock?
    ☐ Yes   ☐ No   ☐ Don't know

16. Were you adopted?   ☐ Yes   ☐ No   ☐ Don't know
    If yes, at what age?
    If yes, do you know your natural parents?   ☐ Yes   ☐ No

17. Was your mother in trauma during pregnancy with you?
    ☐ Yes   ☐ No   ☐ Don't know

18. Were you and your mother bonded at birth?
    ☐ Yes   ☐ No   ☐ Don't know

19. Are your parents living?
    Father   ☐ Yes   ☐ No
    Mother   ☐ Yes   ☐ No
    If no, how old were you when he and/or she died?

20. Are your parents Christians?
    Father   ☐ Yes   ☐ No   ☐ Don't know
    Mother   ☐ Yes   ☐ No   ☐ Don't know

21. In whose home(s) were you raised?

    ☐ Both biological parents'   ☐ Grandparent's home
          home   ☐ Orphanage
    ☐ Adoptive parents' home   ☐ Foster home(s)
    ☐ Mother's home   ☐ Friend's home
    ☐ Father's home   ☐ Other relative's home

22. Were you raised in a Christian home?   ☐ Yes   ☐ No

23. Was (is) your father:
    ☐ Passive   ☐ Strong and manipulative   ☐ Neither

    Would you say you had a good relationship with your
    father?   ☐ Yes   ☐ No

    Would your father say you had a good relationship with
    him?   ☐ Yes   ☐ No   ☐ Don't know

Briefly describe your past and present relationship with your father.

24. Was (is) your mother:
□ Passive   □ Strong and manipulative   □ Neither

Would you say you had a good relationship with your mother?   □ Yes   □ No

Would your mother say you had a good relationship with her?   □ Yes   □ No   □ Don't know

Briefly describe your past and present relationship with your mother.

25. Was your upbringing in an alcoholic or drug-dominated home?   □ Yes   □ No
If yes, please explain briefly.

26. Do you have brothers or sisters?   □ Yes   □ No

Names:

1. _____ Age _____
□ brother   □ sister   □ full   □ half   □ step

2. _____ Age _____
□ brother   □ sister   □ full   □ half   □ step

3. _____ Age _____
□ brother   □ sister   □ full   □ half   □ step

4. _____ Age _____
□ brother   □ sister   □ full   □ half   □ step

5. _____ Age _____
□ brother   □ sister   □ full   □ half   □ step

6. _____ Age _____
□ brother   □ sister   □ full   □ half   □ step

27. Where did you fall in the sibling line?

28. Briefly describe your relationship with your siblings while you were growing up.

29. Briefly describe your relationship with your siblings today.

30. Was yours a happy home during childhood?
    ☐ Yes   ☐ No

31. Were you lonely as a teenager?   ☐ Yes   ☐ No

    Explain briefly.

32. How would you describe your family's financial situation when you were a child?
    ☐ Poor   ☐ Below average   ☐ Average
    ☐ Above average   ☐ Highly affluent

    Do you tithe?   ☐ Yes   ☐ No

33. Was (is) your father a perfectionist?   ☐ Yes   ☐ No

34. Was (is) your mother a perfectionist?   ☐ Yes   ☐ No

35. Were you raised in a physically or verbally abusive home?
    ☐ Yes   ☐ No
    If yes, please explain briefly.

36. Were you sexually abused at home?   ☐ Yes   ☐ No
    If yes, please explain briefly.

37. Were you ever sexually abused outside the home?
    ☐ Yes   ☐ No
    If yes, please explain briefly.

38. Have you, your spouse, your parents or your grandparents been in any of the following cults?

☐ Occultism   ☐ Religious communes
☐ Rosicrucianism   ☐ Theosophy
☐ Jehovah's Witnesses   ☐ Native religions
☐ Gurus   ☐ Unification Church
☐ Unity   ☐ Islam
☐ Spiritist churches   ☐ Hinduism
☐ Children of Love   ☐ Buddhism
☐ Christadelphians   ☐ Christian Science
☐ Scientology   ☐ Mormons
☐ Bahai   ☐ Others

If you checked any of the above, state which relative(s) was involved, when involvement occurred and to what extent.

39. Have you, your spouse, your parents or your grandparents been members of any of the following?

☐ Freemasonry   ☐ Shriners
   (Masonic Lodges)   ☐ Elks Club
☐ Odd Fellows   ☐ DeMolay
☐ Rainbow Girls   ☐ Job's Daughters
☐ Ku Klux Klan   ☐ Daughter of the Nile
☐ Eastern Star   ☐ Others

If you checked any of the above, state which relative(s) was involved, when involvement occurred and to what extent.

40. Have you, your spouse, your parents or your grandparents suffered from any of the following?

☐ High fever   ☐ Allergies
☐ Arthritis   ☐ Impotency
☐ Cancer   ☐ Bent body
☐ Viral infections   ☐ Multiple sclerosis
☐ Asthma   ☐ Muscular dystrophy
☐ Hay fever   ☐ Diabetes

☐ Blindness   ☐ Drug dependence
☐ Blood disease   ☐ Prescription tranquilizer
☐ Lingering disorders   dependence
☐ Mental problems   ☐ Others
☐ Alcoholism

If you checked any of the above, state which relative(s) had these afflictions, when afflicted and to what extent.

41. Did either of your parents suffer from depression?
     ☐ Father   ☐ Mother   ☐ Neither

     If yes for either or both, describe the depression and its impact at home.

Questions about Yourself

42. Are you easily frustrated?   ☐ Yes   ☐ No
     If yes, do you show it or bury it?   ☐ Show   ☐ Bury
     If yes, state what frustrates you.

43. Would you describe yourself as:
     ☐ Anxious   ☐ A worrier   ☐ Depressed

44. Have you ever had psychiatric counseling?   ☐ Yes   ☐ No
     If yes, when?

45. Have you ever been hypnotized?   ☐ Yes   ☐ No

46. Do you feel mentally confused?   ☐ Yes   ☐ No

47. Do you daydream or have mental fantasies?
     ☐ Yes   ☐ No

48. Do you suffer from frequent bad dreams or nightmares?
     ☐ Yes   ☐ No

Describe any recurring themes.

49. Have you ever been tempted to commit suicide?
    ☐ Yes ☐ No
    If yes, when and why?

50. Have you tried to commit suicide? ☐ Yes ☐ No
    If yes, how, when and why?

51. Have you ever wished to die? ☐ Yes ☐ No

52. Have you been involved in occultism or witchcraft?
    ☐ Yes ☐ No

53. Have you ever had involvement with any of the following?

    ☐ Fortunetellers   ☐ White magic
    ☐ Tarot cards   ☐ Demon worship
    ☐ Ouija boards   ☐ Spirit guides
    ☐ Séances   ☐ Clairvoyance
    ☐ Mediums   ☐ Crystals
    ☐ Palmistry   ☐ Automatic handwriting
    ☐ Astrology   ☐ Native healers
    ☐ Color therapy   ☐ Dungeons & Dragons or
    ☐ Levitation   similar games
    ☐ Astral travel   ☐ New Age movement
    ☐ Horoscopes   ☐ Witch doctors
    ☐ Lucky charms   ☐ Voodoo
    ☐ Black magic   ☐ Others

    Describe your involvement with any of the above.

54. Have you ever read books on occultism or witchcraft?
    ☐ Yes ☐ No
    If yes, what and why?

55. Have you made any pacts with Satan? ☐ Yes ☐ No

56. Do you know of any curse placed on you or your family?
☐ Yes ☐ No
If yes, when, by whom and why?

57. Have you been involved with Transcendental Meditation?
☐ Yes ☐ No

58. Have you been involved with Eastern religions?
☐ Yes ☐ No

59. Have you ever visited heathen temples? ☐ Yes ☐ No

60. Have you ever done any form of yoga? ☐ Yes ☐ No

61. Have you learned or used mind communication or mind control? ☐ Yes ☐ No

62. Have you ever seen a demonic presence? ☐ Yes ☐ No
If yes, explain briefly.

63. Do you currently have in your home any symbols of idols or spirit worship like the following?
☐ Buddha   ☐ Pagan symbols
☐ Totem poles   ☐ Tikis
☐ Painted facemasks   ☐ Native art
☐ Idol carvings   ☐ Kachina dolls
☐ Fetish objects or
   feathers

64. With what type of music did you occupy your mind before conversion?
☐ Rock & Roll   ☐ Country
☐ Punk rock   ☐ Gospel/Christian
☐ New Age   ☐ Classical
☐ Rap   ☐ Contemporary
☐ Heavy metal

65. With what type of music do you occupy your mind now?

☐ Rock & Roll   ☐ Country
☐ Punk rock   ☐ Gospel/Christian
☐ New Age   ☐ Classical
☐ Rap   ☐ Contemporary
☐ Heavy metal

66. Have you ever learned any of the martial arts?
☐ Yes   ☐ No

If yes, describe and explain.

67. Have you ever had premonitions, déjà vu or psychic sight?   ☐ Yes   ☐ No

If yes, describe and explain.

68. Do you have any tattoos?   ☐ Yes   ☐ No

69. Have you ever utilized any of the following drugs?

☐ LSD   ☐ Uppers
☐ Speed   ☐ Downers
☐ Marijuana   ☐ Other drugs (list)_____
☐ Cocaine   _____
☐ Crack   _____

Were you addicted?   ☐ Yes   ☐ No

70. Have you ever been addicted to any of the following?

☐ Gambling   ☐ Coffee
☐ Compulsive exercise   ☐ Shopping
☐ Being a spendthrift   ☐ Pornography
☐ Television   ☐ Sex
☐ Alcohol   ☐ Prescription drugs (list)___
☐ Smoking   _____
☐ Food   _____

For questions 71 through 86 please write P for past, C for current or PC for both.

71. In my Christian experience I
___have trouble accepting the deity of Christ.
___have trouble accepting Christ's atoning sacrifice.
___have trouble accepting the teachings of Christ.
___tend to suppress ministries unknowingly.
___tend to gravitate toward humanistic thinking.
___tend to have lawlessness about me.
___do not believe I have an anointing on my life.
___tend often to be under heretical teaching.
___seem always to be persecuted in my walk with Christ.
___have trouble accepting God's forgiveness.

72. I struggle with the following:

___Lust
___Satanic interest
___Various forms of corruption
___My ambitions and achievements
___Fear of death
___Bitterness
___Oppression
___Spiritual blindness
___Control over life
___Religion
___A bound mind
___Spiritual deadness

73. I experience problems in the following areas:

___Mental illness
___Ear maladies
___Near-drowning
___Spiritual deafness or blindness
___Crippled
___Excessive crying or tearing
___Foaming at the mouth
___Alzheimer's
___Gnashing of teeth
___Pining away
___Burns
___Chemical imbalance
___Prostration
___Suicide
___Self-mutilation
___Madness
___Insanity
___Retardation
___Senility
___Schizophrenia

___Seizures   ___Attention deficit
___Epilepsy   ___Eating disorders
___Paranoia   (types)_____
___Hearing voices   _____
___Hallucinations   _____
___Palsy   _____

74. I experience problems in the following areas:

___Death seems to be   ___Death to ministry
   lurking nearby   ___Death in
___Disease   relationships
___Suicide   ___Death in marriage
___Clumsiness   ___Accidents
___Fighting   ___Random acts of
___Daredevil acts   violence
___Speeding

75. I experience interest in the following areas:

___Divination   ___Self-will
___False prophecy   ___Mind control/
___Fortune-telling or   manipulation
   soothsaying   ___Warlock
___Stargazing, zodiac,   ___Witch
   horoscopes   ___Sorcerer
___Rebellion   ___Wizard
___Hypnotist-   ___Spirit guide
   enchanter   ___Vampire
___Acupuncture   ___Animal guide
___Birth charts   ___Astral projection
___Magic (black or   ___Water witching
   white)   ___Lust for power or
___Spiritism   control

76. I struggle with the following areas:

___Error in doctrine   ___Hyper-spirituality
___False prophecy   ___Twisting of
___An unsubmissive   Scripture
   attitude   ___Unteachable spirit

___Mixing the holy
with the profane
___Defensive
___Argumentative
___New Age
movement
___Contentiousness
___Servant to
corruption
___Maintaining a form
of godliness
___Mental confusion
___Fear
___Dullness of
comprehension
___Hindrance to
prayer

___Hindrance to Bible
study
___Hindrance to hear-
ing sermons
___Hindrance to
movement of the
Holy Spirit
___Hindrance to
believing faith
principles
___False doc-
trines such as
Mormonism,
Catholicism,
Buddhism,
Hinduism,
Unitarianism

77. I have involvement in the following areas:

___Familiar spirits
___Divination
___Witchcraft
___Calling on
mediums
___Yoga
___Clairvoyance
___Inferiority
___Mind-dreaming
___Spirit guides/
animal guides

___False prophecy
___Séances
___Bigotry
___Racism
___Low self-esteem
___Peeping and
muttering
___Self-pity
___Necromancy
___Drugs

78. I struggle with the following:

___Fear
___Torment, horror
___Fear of death
___Introversion
___A desire to be a
hermit or recluse

___Anxiety, stress
___Extroversion
___Fear of saying no
___Lack of trust
___Doubt or worry
___Migraines

___Fear of rejection
___Fear of abandonment
___Fear of heart attacks
___Fear of authority
___Fear of failure
___Fear of heights
___A constant desire to be alone
___A critical spirit

___Unhealthy fear of God
___Fear of spiders
___Fear of not being good enough
___Fear of animals
___Panic attacks
___Other fears (list)___
_____
_____
_____

79. I struggle with the following:

___Haughtiness
___Religious pride
___Rationalizing pride
___Scornful attitude
___Vanity
___Professional pride
___Regional pride
___Obstinacy
___National pride
___Self-righteousness
___Dictatorial nature
___Controlling
___Overbearing or domineering
___Manipulating
___Rejection of God's authority
___Rejection of man's authority
___Rebellion

___A holier-than-thou attitude
___Exalted feelings
___Gossiping
___Egotistical attitude
___Self-deception
___Contentiousness
___Bragging and boastful attitude
___Strife
___Idleness
___Performance orientation
___Attention-seeking
___Interrupting others
___Impatience
___Always-right type of attitude
___Being arrogant and smug

80. I struggle with the following:

___Self-hate
___Self-pity
___A broken heart

___Many regrets
___Life's unfairness
___Suicidal thoughts

___Depression
___Excessive
mourning
___Inner hurts and a
torn spirit
___Gluttony
___Loneliness
___Dejection
___Continuous sorrow
and grief
___Discouragement

___Despair
___Hopelessness
___Rejection
___Insecurity
___Abandonment
___Inferiority
___Low self-esteem
___Suppressed
emotions
___Insomnia
___False responsibility

81. I suffer from the following infirmities:

___Infirmity in general
___Bent body, spine
___Chemical
imbalance
___Extended fever
___Impotence
___Frailness
___Lameness
___Arthritis
___Diabetes
___Oppression
___Tuberculosis
___Emphysema
___Excessive pain and
affliction
___Lingering disorders
___Tumors

___Cysts
___Warts
___Excessive fatigue
___Viral infections
___Bacterial infections
___Asthma
___Hay Fever
___Allergies
___Epilepsy
___Seizures
___Leukemia
___Hypochondria
___Cancer (type)_____
_____
_____
_____

82. I struggle with the following:

___Jealousy
___Revenge
___Spite
___Cruelty
___Extreme
competition

___Causing divisions
___Coveting
___Selfishness
___Envy
___Strife
___Contentiousness

___Hatred
___Anger and rage
___Violence
___Bigotry and racism

___Suppressed anger
___Suppressed rage
___Desire to murder

83. I struggle with the following:

___Lying
___Flattery
___Driving zeal
___Strong deception
___False prophecy
___Gossip
___Exaggeration
___False teaching
___Slander
___Accusations
___Religious bondage

___Covenant breaking
___Superstitions
___Profanity
___Guilt
___Shame
___Condemnation
___Melancholy nature
___Self-deception
___False burdens
___Frenzied
emotional actions

84. I struggle with the following:

___Perversity
___Broken spirit
___Evil actions
___Past abortion
___Child abuse
___Prostitution
___Masturbation
___Atheism
___A filthy mind
___Sexual perversion
___Doctrinal error
___Twisting Scripture
___Molestation
___Incest
___Rape
___Date rape
___Spousal rape

___Pornography
___Computer
pornography
___Chronic worry
___Self-love
___Contentiousness
___Foolishness
___Lust
___Homosexuality
___Lesbianism
___Vain imaginations
___Rebellion
___Sexual frigidity
___Emotional frigidity
___Effeminate spirit
___Fornication
___Adultery

85. I struggle with the following:

___Seducing spirits
___Seared conscience
___Deception
___Fascination with
    evil ways
___Seducers
___Enticers
___Fascination with
    evil objects
___Wandering from
    the truth
___Hypocritical lies

___Fascination with
    evil people
___Attraction to false
    signs
___Attraction to false
    prophets
___Attraction to false
    wonders
___Jezebel spirit
___Ahab spirit
    (passivity)

86. I struggle with the following:

___Addiction to
    entertainment
___Unfaithfulness
___Adultery
___Prostitution of
    spirit, soul or body
___Love of money
___Excessive appetite
___Worldliness

___Fornication
___Idolatry
___Chronic
    dissatisfaction
___Love of self
___Self-reward
___Addiction to sports
___Addiction to
    television

87. Please describe as clearly as you can what is going on in
    your life at this time. What prompted you to seek spiritual
    counseling?

_____

_____

_____

_____

_____

_____

_____

_____

_____

_____

Please place a check by each statement that describes how you think about yourself.

88. ___I am all alone.
    ___I have been overlooked.
    ___They do not need me.
    ___I don't matter.
    ___No one ever cares.
    ___They are not coming back.
    ___God has forsaken me, too.
    ___There is no one to protect me.
    ___No one will believe me.
    ___I cannot trust anyone.
    ___I am afraid they won't come back.

89. ___I am so stupid, ignorant, an idiot.
    ___I allowed it.
    ___I was a participant.
    ___I should have known better.
    ___I should have done something to have stopped it from happening.
    ___It was my fault.
    ___I knew what was going to happen, yet I stayed away.
    ___I should have told someone.
    ___I felt pleasure, so I must have wanted it.
    ___It happened because of my looks, my sex, my body, etc.
    ___I should have stopped them.

___I did not try to run away.
___I am cheap like a slut.
___I was paid for services rendered.
___I deserved it.
___I kept going back.
___I did it to him/her first.
___I'm bad, dirty, shameful, sick, nasty.

90. ___I am going to die.
___He/she is going to hurt me.
___I do not know what to do.
___If I tell they will come back and hurt me.
___If I trust I will die.
___He/she/they are coming back.
___It is just a matter of time before it happens again.
___They are going to get me.
___If I let him/her/them into my life, he/she/they will hurt me, too.
___Doom is just around the corner.
___Something bad will happen if I tell, stop it, confront it.

91. ___He/she/they are too strong to resist.
___I cannot stop this.
___I am going to die and I cannot do anything about it.
___There is no way out.
___I am too weak to resist.
___The pain is too great to bear.
___I cannot get away.
___I cannot get loose.
___I am overwhelmed.
___I don't know what to do.
___Everything is out of control.
___I am pulled in every direction.
___Not even God can help me.
___I am too small to do anything.

92. ___I am dirty, evil, shameful, perverted, because of what happened to me.
___My life is ruined.

___No one will really be able to love me.

___I will never be happy.

___Everyone can see my shame, filth, dirtiness, etc.

___I will always be unclean, filthy, etc.

___I will always be hurt/damaged/broken because of what has happened.

___My body parts are dirty.

___God could never want me after what has happened to me.

___I will never feel clean again.

93.   ___I am not loved, needed, cared for or important.

___They do not need me.

___I am worthless and have no value.

___I am unimportant.

___I was a mistake.

___I should have never been born.

___I was never liked by them, because I was _____!

___God could never love or accept me.

___I am in the way; I am a burden.

___I could never be as_____ as he or she is.

___I could never jump high enough to please him/her.

___I am not acceptable.

94.   ___It is never going to get any better.

___There is no way out.

___It will just happen again and again.

___There is no good thing for me.

___I have no reason to live.

___There are no options for me.

___I just want to die.

___Nothing good will ever come of this.

95.   ___I don't know what is happening to me.

___Everything is confusing.

___This does not make any sense.

___Why would they do this to me?

Other Areas of Your Life

96. Do you have known sin, unforgiveness, resentment, bitterness or hatred toward anyone? Toward whom and why? (List all.)

_____

_____

_____

_____

_____

_____

97. Have you been given any type of training about deliverance and inner healing? Have you ever attended a healing retreat that gave you insight into deliverance and inner healing?   ☐ Yes   ☐ No
If yes, describe your experience.

_____

_____

_____

_____

_____

_____

98. Have you ever received prayer for deliverance?
☐ Yes   ☐ No
If yes, describe your experience.

_____

_____

_____

_____

_____

_____

_____

99. Describe your dreams, goals and aspirations for your life.

_____

_____

_____

_____

_____

_____

_____

100. Are there any other problems you feel this questionnaire
has not addressed? Please explain.

_____

_____

_____

_____

_____

How to Use the Questionnaire

A thorough questionnaire has proven to be one of the most valuable tools of personal ministry. It provides a wealth of information that can be used for counseling, inner healing and deliverance. The questionnaire, if filled out completely and honestly, will give the prayer minister a road map to follow that will expose the root causes and entry points of the demonic attacks that people are seeking help for. Following is a brief summary of what areas are exposed by each grouping of questions.

Questions 1–7

These questions inform you about their spiritual background, including their salvation experience. You need to know if they are born again. Do they have a personal relationship with Jesus? Do they know they are saved? Were they involved in any cults or false religions? Are they baptized with the Holy Spirit with evidence of speaking in tongues? I feel a person must be baptized with the Holy Spirit in order to avoid being swept clean, put in order and empty for demons to return in greater force (see Matthew 12:43).

Questions 8–12

These will clue you in on family, ethnic and cultural matters that could have a spiritual effect on persons coming for prayer, such as generational curses. They also reveal any unholy places they may have visited. Many people who go to Asia visit heathen temples and honor the heathen deities by removing their shoes to enter. They may have actually offered sacrifices of some kind and thus brought curses upon themselves. They will need to repent, renounce the god or goddess and break the curse on them.

Questions 13–37

These questions reveal rejection issues as well as possible abuse and neglect issues. You will gain valuable information on their relationships with their fathers. People's relationship or lack of relationship with their earthly fathers is the model for their relationship with their heavenly Father.

If their fathers were distant and seemingly uncaring, they will see God the same way. If they were raised in a home full of drug and alcohol abuse, there will be a strong possibility of spirits of addiction or bondage in their lives. This area will also reveal emotional, physical and sexual abuses in the home.

Note: Children brought up in homes dominated by drugs and alcohol are oftentimes abused physically and sexually. Nine out of ten women we have ministered to in this situation have been abused sexually, usually by a close family member. Many we have counseled had never told anyone, yet many wrote it down when completing the questionnaire. (Remember: Once this is brought out into the light, Satan loses his power in their lives!)

Questions 38–41

In these questions you are looking for generational or family involvement in cults, false religions and secret societies. This also uncovers generational spirits of infirmity.

Questions 42–51

Look here for areas of mental weakness and illness, both of which are demonic. The society we live in, however, tends to consider these as medical issues. *Be warned:* This can put you in a position to be charged in a liability or a malpractice suit. The situation is complicated further if they are taking a mind-altering drug because it might hinder their ability to receive ministry from you. Never proceed with ministry that is beyond your capabilities.

Questions 52–63

These questions expose their personal involvement in witchcraft and the occult. I believe this is a major open door to the demonic, second only to sexual sin. Also, it is the toughest to deal with.

Questions 64–67

The spirit of Antichrist can come into a person through rock music and rap music. Also martial arts are part of Near Eastern religions, and are nothing more than demon worship.

Question 68

Scripture forbids tattoos, yet we see more people sporting them than ever before, especially young people. Satan knows his time is short and he is trying to mark as many people as he can. People need to repent for defiling the temple of the Holy Ghost and for violating Scripture. They then need to renounce any demon the tattoo represents and break any curse that came in as a result. If possible they should consider having the tattoo removed.

Note: There are no such things as Christian tattoos! All tattoos are demonic.

Questions 69–86

These are listings of the fruits and manifestation of various spirits or strongholds. As you look down through these questions you can easily see which areas you will need to focus in on. If there is current involvement, you can rest assured there is either a sin issue or a demonic presence to deal with, or both. Also remember that some folks will put *P* as though the issue was in the past when they are actually still struggling in that area. They are dealing with embarrassment. If an area has a large number of *P*s I would focus in on that area as well. The following is a key to use with the various categories.

69: Bondage and witchcraft
70: All are signs of bondage
71: Fruit of Antichrist spirit
72: All are signs of bondage
73: A deaf and dumb spirit
74: A spirit of death
75: Witchcraft, divination and the occult
76: A spirit of error
77: Familiar spirits
78: The spirit of fear
79: Pride and haughtiness
80: Heaviness and rejection
81: Infirmity, sickness and disease
82: Jealousy and anger
83: A lying spirit
84: A perverse spirit
85: Seducing and deceiving spirits
86: Stronghold of whoredoms

Question 87

This is a good place to start with anyone who comes to you for ministry. Why are you here? More often than not the response will be a fruit of an underlying issue.

Questions 88–95

These are lists of lies people believe about themselves. Following is a list of the areas you will most likely have to minister in, based on the number of lies they believe.

88: Rejection
89: Sexual abuse
90: Fear and abuse
91: Fear and abuse
92: Sexual abuse
93: Rejection
94: Death
95: Error

Question 96

This shows any areas of unforgiveness. These issues must be resolved prior to deliverance.

Question 97

At Righteous Acts Ministries, we recommend that everyone who comes to us for counseling, inner healing or deliverance first complete some kind of training seminar and/or healing retreat experience. I have mentioned Cleansing Stream a number of times in this book; it is an excellent resource in this regard. By going through some experience like this, probably 95 percent of those seeking help will receive their healing or deliverance. We then can minister to the 5 percent of severe or chronic cases. This consumes most of our ministry time. You will find, once you start a counseling and deliverance ministry, that you always have a waiting list.

Question 98

This is an extremely important question. If they have had repeated deliverance sessions with other ministries, and they are still not walking in freedom, there is usually a reason. They may be looking for a quick fix. They may be in sin, thus keeping the door open for the devil. They may have a problem with unforgiveness or bitterness. They may have mental illness or have multiple personality disorder. Or they may be planted by the enemy to distract you. I really look at these folks carefully and prayerfully.

Question 99

The answer given here will let you know how serious they are about God, and give you a good idea of where they are spiritually.

Question 100

This is potluck.

Appendix 2

Prayer for Deliverance

Dear Lord Jesus, I believe that You are the Son of God, that You died on the cross for my sins and that You rose again from the dead. I confess You as my Lord and Savior.

Dear Heavenly Father, You have told us to put on the Lord Jesus Christ and to make no provision for the flesh in regard to its lust. I acknowledge that I have given in to fleshly lusts, which wage war against my soul. I thank You that in Christ my sins are forgiven, but I have transgressed Your holy law and given the enemy an opportunity to wage war in my members. I come before Your presence to acknowledge these sins and to seek Your cleansing that I may be freed from the bondage of sin. I now ask You to reveal to my mind the ways that I have transgressed Your moral law and grieved the Holy Spirit. In Jesus' precious name I pray, amen.

Heavenly Father, I renounce and repent of my sins and the sins of my forefathers and foremothers back to the third, fourth, even the tenth generation and beyond. I break every vex, every hex, every connection with voodoo, all witch-craft, every covenant, every blood covenant, every vow, every oath, every sacrifice, every blood sacrifice, every blood oath and blood vow, every chant, every incantation and every spell. I now break all curses spoken or unspoken. In the mighty name of Jesus and by His blood, I call them powerless. I call them null and void on all past, present and future generations. In Jesus' name, amen.

In the name of Jesus Christ, the name that has all author-ity in heaven and on earth and beneath the earth, I renounce every sinful word I have spoken or thought about You, God, and I ask You to forgive me. In Jesus' name, I break all curses on me due to blasphemy or cursing You by me, my family or prior generations. I forgive all offense that I have taken at what You did or did not do. You are Sovereign, Lord. You alone are Most High God. I love You and do not resist You.

In Jesus' precious name, I renounce every sinful thought or word against any servant of God. I ask Your forgive-ness where I have lifted my hands against Your anointed ones. I forgive all Your servants for giving offense, and I pray Your blessings on every servant of Yours that I have ever known. In Jesus' name, I claim the release of the cross for every curse passed down to me by my family or prior generations for cursing Your servants. The blood of Jesus is between them and me.

In the name of Jesus, the name that is above all names, I renounce and ask You to forgive me for every sin of par-ticipating, willingly or in ignorance, in occult practices, witchcraft, sorcery, spiritism and any other work of the kingdom of darkness. Those sins are nailed to the cross, and the blood of Jesus covers them. There are no unsettled claims on me because of them. All is settled for me in Christ Jesus. I break all curses handed down to me by my family, prior generations or any other person participating in or invoking the occult, witchcraft, sorcery, spiritism or any other work of the kingdom of darkness.

In the name of Jesus, I renounce and ask Your forgiveness for every sin I have committed, spoken, or thought in rebellion, disobedience, weakness or ignorance. In Jesus' name, I break all curses brought on me by these sins.

In the name of the Lord Jesus, I renounce and ask You to forgive me for every sinful word I have spoken or thought about my parents and any act I committed that dishonored my father or mother. I forgive my father and mother for every offense against me. I apply the redemption and release of the cross and break all curses on me brought on by myself, my family or prior generations, due to cursing a father or mother. And I break every judgment I have placed on my mother and father for whatever they did or did not do, in Jesus' name, amen.

I renounce all curses on me handed down by my family or prior generations. I do not choose to practice any sins of my parents or my ancestors. I forgive my parents and ancestors for causing any curse to come upon me.

I repent of all my sins. I repent of all my contacts with Satan and all his evil works. I renounce any involvement with the occult. I repent and renounce all demon spirits that I have allowed to enter my life.

Lord, I forgive all others who have wronged me or harmed me. I lay down all resentment, all hatred and all rebellion. In particular I forgive_____ (name).

Lord, I ask You to forgive me and to cleanse me by Your precious blood. I accept forgiveness now. I accept Your forgiveness and I forgive myself.

Now, Lord, I loose myself from every demon spirit in the name of Jesus and I command them to leave me. Lord, Your Word says that "whosoever shall call on the name of the LORD shall be delivered" (Joel 2:32, KJV). I call on Your name right now, and I recognize You as my deliverer.

Satan, because of the blood of Jesus, you have no power over me and you have no place in me. I now cancel any legal right you have to remain. In the name of Jesus, amen.

Appendix 3

Prayer to Break Soul Ties

Heavenly Father, I ask You to forgive me of any and all sexual misconduct, specifically with _____ (name), and any unnatural or ungodly relationship with any other person, place or thing. And in the mighty name of Jesus, I ask that my spirit be loosed from them according to Matthew 18:18–19. I tell my spirit to forget the unions. I tell my mind to release responsibility for them. I tell my emotions to let go and forget the union. I tell the fragmented pieces of my soul to come back together. I hereby break every soul tie in the name of Jesus. Amen.

Lord, I renounce all uses of my body as an instrument of unrighteousness and by so doing ask You to break all bondage that Satan has brought into my life through that involvement. I confess my participation. I now present my body to You as a living sacrifice, holy and acceptable to You, and I reserve the sexual use of my body only for marriage. I renounce the lie of Satan that my body is not clean, that it is dirty or in any way unacceptable as a result of my past sexual experience.

Lord, I thank You that You have cleansed me totally and have forgiven me, that You love and accept me unconditionally. I can, therefore, accept myself, and I choose to do so—to accept myself and my body as cleansed. In Jesus' name, amen.

(Thanks to Teresa Castleman for the basis of this prayer.)

Appendix 4

Prayer to Break Curses of Death

I renounce and break every curse of premature death and I break every assignment of the enemy against my life, including:

- Accidents
- Random acts of violence
- Disease
- Cancer
- Suicide
- Clumsiness
- Fighting
- Daredevil acts
- Speeding
- Murder

I break every assignment of:

- Abortion
- Miscarriage

I also renounce and break every assignment of death to my:

- Ministry
- Relationships
- Marriage
- Spiritual life
- Emotions
- Finances

And I renounce and break off any familiar spirit of death in Jesus' name, amen.

(Note: If a spirit of death manifests, cast it out. Its assignment is broken.)

Appendix 5

Prayer to Break Vietnam Curses

I break all curses spoken by any Buddhist monks over myself and my family that could cause me:

- Never to find peace
- Always to be angry
- To have a wandering spirit

I also break all soul ties and any curses or transference of spirits from any and all prostitutes in Jesus' name, amen.

Appendix 6

Strongholds,
Their Manifestations and Fruit

Through the name of Jesus we have authority to cast out demons and pull down strongholds. He has given us dominion and authority. As we move in that power we can and will be more than conquerors over the power of the enemy.

The pages that follow list numerous strongholds and the way that they manifest in humans. A person receiving prayer ministry can use this information to renounce these works of darkness.

Stronghold of Antichrist

1 John 4:3

I renounce the stronghold of Antichrist, every spirit of Antichrist and its manifestations and fruit.

I renounce:

- Any spirit that:
  - Denies the deity of Christ
  - Denies the atonement
  - Comes against Christ and His teaching
  - Suppresses ministries

- Secular humanism
- Jezebel spirit
- Worldly speech and actions
- Profanity
- Anti-Christianity
- Lawlessness
- The accuser
- The deceiver
- Any serpent spirit
- A dragon spirit
- Rock music, rap music or any ungodly music
- Legalism, ritualism or formalism
- Teachers of heresies
  - Mormonism
  - Catholicism
  - Pharisaism
  - Unitarianism
  - Nazism
  - Communism
  - Buddhism
  - Hinduism
  - New Age beliefs
  - Freemasonry

- Familiar spirit of Antichrist
- _____
- _____
- _____
- _____

Stronghold of Bondage

Romans 8:15

I renounce the stronghold of bondage and its manifestations and fruit.

I renounce:

- Bondage to fear
- Bondage to all addictions:
  - Drugs
  - Alcohol
  - Cigarettes
  - Food
  - Sex
  - TV
  - Computers
  - Shopping, etc.
- Bondage to lust
- A bound spirit
- A mind-binding spirit
- Bondage to sin
- Compulsive behavior
- Compulsive sin
- Captivity to Satan
- Servant to corruption

- Religious bondage
- Idolatry
- Bondage to ambition and achievement
- Bondage to bitterness
- Bondage to oppression
- Spiritual blindness
- Fear of death
- Spiritual death
- Control
- Familiar spirit of bondage
- _____
- _____
- _____
- _____

Stronghold of a Deaf and Dumb Spirit

Mark 9:25

I renounce the deaf and dumb spirit and its manifestations and fruit.

I renounce:

- Being dumb and mute
- Deafness/spiritual deafness
- Blindness/spiritual blindness
- Drowning
- Compulsive behavior
- Mental illness
- Madness
- Insanity
- Retardation

- Senility
- Schizophrenia
- Paranoia
- Hearing voices
- Hallucinations
- Palsy
- ADD, ADHD
- MPD
- Crippling
- Crying and tearing
- Ear problems
- Foaming at the mouth
- Alzheimer's
- Gnashing of teeth
- Pining away
- Prostration
- Burns
- Suicidal tendencies
- Chemical imbalance
- Seizures and epilepsy
- Self-hatred
- Self-mutilation
- Eating disorders
- Familiar spirit of deaf and dumb
- _____
- _____
- _____
- _____

Stronghold of Death

1 Corinthians 15:26

I renounce the spirit of death and the curse of premature death. I break all plans of the enemy and I break every assignment against my life due to:

- Accidents
- Random acts of violence
- Disease
- Cancer
- Suicide
- Clumsiness
- Fighting
- Daredevil acts
- Speeding

I break every assignment of:

- Abortion
- Miscarriages

And I break every assignment of death to my:

- Ministry
- Anointing
- Relationships
- Marriage
- Familiar spirit of death
- _____
- _____
- _____
- _____

Stronghold of Divination

Acts 16:16

I renounce the stronghold of divination and witchcraft and its manifestations and fruit.
I renounce:

- Lust for power and control
- Fortunetellers, soothsayers and psychics
- Stargazer, zodiac and horoscopes
- False prophets
- Warlock, witch, sorcerer and wizard
- All spirit guides
- All animal guides
- All Indian witchcraft
- Astral projection
- Druid and Celtic witchcraft
- Occultism
- Rebellion
- Hypnotist and enchanter
- Acupuncture
- Drugs
- Birth charts
- All magic, black or white
- A serpent spirit
- A vampire spirit
- Spiritist
- Jezebel
- Water witching
- Divination
- Self-will

- Mind-control
- Manipulation
- Automatic handwriting, and handwriting analysis
- Wicca
- Familiar spirit of divination and witchcraft
- _____
- _____
- _____
- _____

The Stronghold of Error

1 John 4:6

I renounce the stronghold of error and its manifestation and fruit.
    I renounce:

- A spirit of error
- All false prophecies spoken over me by anyone, including myself
- Unsubmissiveness
- Hyper-spirituality
- All false doctrines
    - Mormonism
    - Catholicism
    - Pharisaism
    - Buddhism
    - Hinduism
    - Freemasonry
    - New Age movement
    - Unitarianism

- Communism
- Nazism
- Twisting Scripture
- An unteachable spirit
- Mixing the holy with the profane
- A defensive and argumentative spirit
- Sympathy for the devil
- Contentions
- Servant of corruption
- Having a form of godliness but denying its power
- Mental confusion and fears
- Physical illness and pain
- Depression
- Dullness of comprehension
- Spiritual hindrances to:
  - Prayer
  - Bible study
  - Listening to services
  - Moving in the gifts of the Spirit
- Faith principles that have come in through error
- Familiar spirit of error
- _____
- _____
- _____
- _____

Stronghold of a Familiar Spirit

Leviticus 19:31

I renounce all familiar spirits, all knowing spirits and generational spirits and their manifestations and fruit.

I renounce the familiar spirit of:

- Fear
- Death
- Antichrist
- Bondage
- Haughtiness
- Heaviness
- Whoredom
- Seduction
- Deaf and dumb
- Jealousy
- Perversion
- Lying
- Infirmity
- Divination
- Error
- Inferiority and low self-esteem
- Bigotry and racism
- Self-pity

I also renounce:

- Necromancy
- Mediums and wizardry
- Yoga and all mantras
- Clairvoyance
- Spiritists
- Passive mind-dreamers
- Spirit guides and animal guides
- All false prophecies
- Drugs

- The deceiver
- The tormentor
- Divorce
- Abortion
- _____
- _____
- _____

Stronghold of Fear

2 Timothy 1:7

I renounce the stronghold of fear and its manifestations and fruit.
I renounce:

- A spirit of fear
- A critical spirit
- Mistrust
- Doubt
- Worry
- Unbelief
- Anxiety
- Stress
- Panic attacks
- Migraines
- Torment
- Horror
- Terror
- Nightmares
- Fear of the dark

- Fear of death
  - Death to self
  - Death to family
- Hermit and recluse
- Introversion
- An alone spirit
- Fear of man
- Fear of relationships
- Fear of molestation or rape
- Fear of rejection
- Fear of abandonment
- Extroversion
- Heart attacks
- Fear of authority
- Fear of saying no
- Fear of failure
- Perfectionism
- Not being good enough
- Fear of food
- Unhealthy fear of God
- All phobias
  - Heights
  - Animals
  - Spiders
  - Water, etc.
- Fear that came in from horror movies
- Fear of not having fear
- _____
- _____
- _____
- _____

Stronghold of Haughtiness

Proverbs 16:18

I renounce the stronghold of haughtiness and its manifestations and fruit.
I renounce:

- Arrogance, smugness
- Vain, vanity
- Pride
- Rationalization in the area of pride
- Professional pride
- National pride
- Regional pride
- Bragging and boastfulness
- Egotism
- Scorn
- Obstinacy
- Self-righteousness
- Being dictatorial and controlling
- Being overbearing and domineering
- Manipulation and control
- Rejection of God and rejection of authority
- Rebellion
- A holier-than-thou attitude
- Exalted feelings
- Gossip
- Division
- Dissension
- Contentiousness
- Strife

- Self-deception
- Idleness
- Performance mentality
- Attention seekers and demonstrativeness
- Interruptions
- Impatience
- Always being right
- Being critical and fault-finding
- Haughtiness that came in through abuse and hurts
- Familiar spirit of haughtiness
- _____
- _____

Stronghold of Heaviness

Isaiah 61:3

I renounce the stronghold of heaviness and its manifestations and fruit.
I renounce:

- The sorrow and grief
- Self-pity
- A broken heart
- Inner hurts and a torn spirit
- Regrets from the unfairness of life
  (Note: Pull regrets from their memory recall.)

- False responsibility
- Suicidal thoughts
- Gluttony
- Loneliness
- Heaviness and depression

- Excessive mourning
- Discouragement and despair
- Dejection and hopelessness
- Rejection, insecurity and abandonment
- Inferiority and low self-esteem
- Lack of praise and unpacified emotions
- Suppressed emotions of fear, anger, rage, violence and hatred
- Self-hatred
- Self-mutilation
- Insomnia
- Chemical imbalance
- Results of sexual abuse
- Familiar spirit of heaviness
- _____
- _____
- _____
- _____

I renounce the spirit of rejection that entered:

- In the womb
- During childbirth (through traumas)
- By not bonding with my mother at birth
- Through adoption or the threat of adoption
- Through childhood hurts and abuses at home or at school
- Through divorce
- Through death
- By betrayal or a broken engagement
- By loss of a job
- Through depression

- Through guilt or shame
- Through abandonment
- Through a familiar spirit of rejection
- _____
- _____
- _____

Stronghold of Infirmity

Luke 13:11

I renounce the stronghold of infirmity and its manifestations and fruit. And I break every assignment, past, present and future.
I renounce:

- Hypochondria
- A bent body and spine
- Chemical imbalance
- High fever
- All mental illness
- Bipolar disorder
- Impotence—frail and lame
- Arthritis and a root of bitterness
- Diabetes
- All oppression
- Pain and affliction
- All lingering disorders
- TB and emphysema
- Cancer
- Tumors and cysts
- Weakness, tiredness and fatigue

- All infections (viral and bacterial)
- Asthma, allergies and hay fever
- Epilepsy and seizures
- Fear of infirmity, sickness and disease
- Familiar spirit of infirmity, sickness and disease
- _____
- _____
- _____
- _____

Stronghold of Jealousy

Proverbs 6:34

I renounce the stronghold of jealousy and its manifestations and fruit.
I renounce:

- Jealousy
- Murder
- Revenge and spite
- Cruelty
- Extreme competition
- Causing divisions
- Coveting
- Selfishness
- Envy
- Strife
- Contention
- Hatred
- Anger and rage
- Violence

- Bigotry and racism
- Vigilante attitude
- Suppressed anger and rage
- Familiar spirit of jealousy
- _____
- _____

Stronghold of Lying

2 Chronicles 18:22

I renounce the stronghold of lying and its manifestations and fruit. I break all false prophecies and the power of the words spoken over me.
  I renounce:

- Strong deception
- Self-deception
- Gossip
- Flattery
- Exaggeration
- False memories
- Lies from false teachers
- All lies, white and black
- Slander
- Accusations
- Religious bondage
- Superstition and old wives' tales
- Profanity
- Guilt, shame and condemnation
- Homosexuality, bisexuality and lesbianism
- Melancholy spirit

- False burdens
- Driving zeal
- Covenant breaking
- Frenzied emotional actions
- Familiar spirit of lying
- _____
- _____
- _____
- _____

Stronghold of Perverseness

Isaiah 19:14

I renounce the stronghold of perverseness and its manifestations and fruit.
I renounce:

- Lying
- A broken spirit
- Uncleanness and lewdness
- Evil actions
- Abortion
- Child abuse and molestation
- Incest—physical and emotional
- Prostitution of body, soul, spirit
- Masturbation and self-gratification
- Exposure and voyeurism
- Atheism
- Filthy mind
- Sexual perversions
- Doctrinal error

- Twisting Scripture
- Satanic ritual abuse
- Ritual molestation and rape
- Satanic dedications and marriage ceremonies
- Rape
- Sodomy
- Pornography
- Chronic worry
- Self-love
- Egocentric thinking
- Contentiousness and foolishness
- Lust
- Homosexuality and lesbianism
- Bisexuality and bestiality
- Sadomasochism
- Vain imagination and fantasy lust
- Frigid spirit (sexual or emotional)
- Effeminate spirit (male)
- Masculine spirit (female)
- Fornication and adultery
- All sexual demons, including
  - Incubus
  - Succubus
- Familiar spirit of perversion
- _____
- _____
- _____
- _____

Stronghold of a Seducing Spirit

1 Timothy 4:1

I renounce the stronghold of seducing and deceiving spirits and their manifestations and fruit.

I renounce:

- A seared conscience
- All deception
- A vigilante spirit
- All fascination with
  - Evil ways
  - Evil objects
  - Evil persons
- Seducers and enticers
- Wandering from the truth
- Hypocritical lies
- All attractions and fascination by
  - False prophets
  - Signs and wonders, etc.
- A Jezebel spirit
- An Ahab spirit
- Familiar spirit of seduction and enticement
- _____
- _____
- _____
- _____

Stronghold of Whoredoms

Hosea 5:4

I renounce the stronghold of prostitution and whoredom and its manifestations and fruit.
I renounce:

- All unfaithfulness
- Adultery
- Fornication
- Prostitution of spirit, soul, body
- Love of money
- Materialism
- Love of control
- Love of power
- Excessive appetites
- Worldliness
- Worldly speech and actions
- Idolatry
- Chronic dissatisfaction
- Love of self
- Self-reward
- Familiar spirit of whoredom
- _____
- _____
- _____
- _____

Appendix 7

Blessings

In the name of Jesus Christ, I bless you _____
(name) with the promises of God, which are yes and amen.
I pray the Holy Spirit will make you healthy and strong in
body, mind and spirit to move in faith and expectancy. May
God's angels be with you to protect and keep you.

- God bless you with ability, with abundance and with
  an assurance of His love and grace.
- God bless you with clear direction, with a controlled
  and disciplined life.
- God bless you with courage and creativity.
- God bless you with spiritual perception of His
  truth.
- God bless you with great faith, and with His favor
  and with man's.
- God bless you with good health and a good _____
  ___ (wife or husband).

- God bless your hands to bless others.
- God bless you with happiness, fulfillment, contentment, hope and a good outlook on life.
- God bless you with a listening ear and with long life and an obedient heart to the Spirit of God.
- God bless you with His peace, with pleasant speech, a pleasant personality, with promotion, protection, provision, safety and strength.
- God bless you with success, trust and wisdom.
- God bless you with goodness and mercy following you all the days of your life that you might dwell in the house of the Lord forever.

The Lord bless you and keep you. The Lord make His face to shine upon you and give you peace, the peace of God that surpasses all understanding. I bless you, _____ (name), in the name of Jesus Christ. Amen.

(Thanks to Teresa Castleman for the basis of this prayer.)

Appendix 8

Staying Free

Deliverance is not the end, it is the beginning. We receive deliverance from past hurts, wounds and bondage, and then we press on toward the goal. As we do so, we need to understand that no matter what our nationality or where we are from, we have a new citizenship. We are no longer of this world; our citizenship is in heaven and we are just pilgrims passing through this world. Knowing this will help us to keep our focus on the goal. We should also note that the enemy is not going to give up. There will still be temptations, trials, tests and attacks. When we are under attack, we need to know that this, too, will pass. Everything in life is temporal.

We know from Jesus' words in Matthew 12:43–45 that an evil spirit will try to return to the "house" from which it was cast out. We want to make sure that if and when that spirit returns, it finds that house full of the Holy Spirit and the power of God. To do this we must be baptized in the Holy Spirit and we must be full of the Word of God.

We also know from Jesus' words to the man at the pool of Bethesda (see John 5:1–15) that a return to sin, after deliverance, can mean a return to an even worse state. Most bondage comes in through sin, and most spirits and strongholds are fed by sin. To walk out our deliverance and to stay free we, too, must go and sin no more. That points also to the importance of breaking any bad habits. To walk in freedom we have to choose to walk in the truth.

Anyone who has not been water baptized needs to be. Statistically, most new Christians who backslide were never baptized. Baptism is a command, not an option. The next thing is to get tied into a good church and become accountable to someone—a cell group leader, a pastor or a mature Christian brother or sister.

Lastly, we must not wait for the enemy to attack; the best defense is a good offense! We have to get into the Word, pray every day and put on the full armor of God according to Ephesians 6. We must guard our thoughts. We are what we think. The battlefield is the mind. We must take authority over it, walk in freedom and stay free.

Here are a few paraphrases of Scripture to confess in this new walk of freedom.

My body is a temple for the Holy Spirit, redeemed, cleansed and sanctified by the blood of Jesus. The devil has no place in me, no power over me, no unsettled claims against me. All has been settled by the blood of Jesus. I overcome Satan by the blood of the Lamb and by the word of my testimony. (See Romans 8:33–34; 1 Corinthians 6:19; Ephesians 1:7; Hebrews 13:12; 1 John 1:7, Revelation 12:11.)

I am not under guilt or condemnation. There is no condemnation for those in Christ Jesus. Satan is a liar. I will not listen to his accusations. No weapon formed against me will prosper. (See Isaiah 54:17; Romans 8:1.)

My mind is being renewed by the Word of God. I pull down strongholds, I cast down imaginations and I bring every thought captive to the obedience of Christ. I resist the devil and he must flee from me now! (See Romans 12:2; 2 Corinthians 10:4; James 4:7–8.)

I give no place to fear in my life. The fear of man brings a snare, but perfect love casts out fear. I sought the Lord and He heard me and delivered me from all my fears. (See Psalm 34:4; 2 Timothy 1:7; 1 John 4:18.)

The Lord is my light and my salvation; whom shall I fear? The Lord is the strength of my life; of whom shall I be afraid? God is my refuge and strength. God will never fail me nor forsake me. (See Psalm 27:1; Psalm 46:1–2; Hebrews 13:5.)

Notes

Chapter 1: Deliverance: The End-Time Ministry

1. "Vatican Issues First New Exorcism Ritual Since 1614," CNN, January 26, 1999, www.cnn.com/WORLD/europe/9901/26/exorcism.

2. "John Paul II Helps Possessed Woman in Vatican," *Zenit News Agency*, September 10, 2000, www.zenit.org/english/archive/0009/ZE000910.html.

3. Ibid.

4. Francis T. Hurley, "Exorcism," *World Book Online*, Americas Edition, www.cssvc.worldbook.compuserve.com/wbol/wbPage/na/ar/co/188560.

5. For these and other statistics gathered by Teen Mania, see the website at www.teenmania.com.

6. Please see the American Academy of Pediatrics website at www.aap.org/family/tv1.htm.

7. Please see the National Institute on Media and the Family website at www.mediafamily.org/research/report.

8. Ibid.

9. Please see the National Council for Missing and Exploited Children website at www.missingkids.com.

Chapter 2: Can a Christian Be "Possessed"?

1. Graham Cooke, *Developing Your Prophetic Gifting* (Kent, England: Renew Publishing, 1994), 225.

Chapter 3: Our Calling and Anointing in Christ

1. Dr. Ron Mosley, *Yeshua, A Guide to the Real Jesus and the Original Church* (Baltimore, Md.: Leader/Messianic Jewish Publishers, 1996).

2. Matthew Henry, *A Commentary on the Whole Bible*, vol. 5, *Matthew to John* (Old Tappan, N.J.: Revell, 1983), 572.

3. P. J. Toner, *The Catholic Encyclopedia*, trans. Joseph P. Thomas (Online edition: K. Knight, 2003), www.newadvent.org/cathen/05711a.htm.

4. Ibid.

5. Ibid.

6. Ibid.

7. Philip Schaff, *History of the Christian Church*, vols. 2, 3 (Peabody, Mass.: Hendrickson, 1996).

8. Sinclair B. Ferguson, David F. Wright, and J. I. Packer, *New Dictionary of Theology* (Downers Grove, Ill.: InterVarsity, 1988).

9. Albert Barnes, *Barnes' Notes on the New Testament* (Grand Rapids: Baker, 1980).

Chapter 4: Reality of the Spirit Realm

1. Online daily devotionals by Neil Anderson can be found at his Crosswalk .com website: www.crosswalk.com/faith/devotionals/dailyinchrist/.

Chapter 5: Sin: The Number One Open Door

1. Annett Nay, "Brownies with a Difference!" *Life in the Word* (May 2000): 12.

Chapter 6: Curses: Five Sources

1. This is from a teaching by Jack Hayford on "The Power of Words" given at a Cleansing Stream Ministries seminar in Van Nuys, California, in 1997.

2. For an interesting corroboration see Ian Wilson's *The Shroud of Turin* (New York: Doubleday, 1979).

3. W. E. Vine, *An Expository Dictionary of Biblical Words* (Nashville: Nelson, 1984), 993.

Chapter 7: Witchcraft and the Occult

1. The Rev. David Hogan told me about this incident when I was with him in south central Mexico in 1998.

2. Courtney McBath, "Is the Anointing For Sale?" *Charisma and Christian Life* (October 2001), 69.

3. William Schnoebelen, *Wicca, Satan's Little White Lie* (Chino, Calif.: Chick Publications, 1990), 1.

4. Margot Adler, *Drawing Down the Moon* (New York: Viking, 1979), 113.

5. This is from material labeled "Modern Witchcraft" on the Pagan Educational Network (PEN), www.bloomington.in.us/~pen/mwcraft.html.

6. Ibid.

7. This prayer for release from the curses of Freemasonry can be found at the Jubilee Resources International website: www.jubilee.org.nz.

8. "Prayers of Release for Freemasons and Their Descendants" can be found in our companion publication *The Deliverance Training Manual*. The manual is available directly through our ministry: William Sudduth, Deliverance Training

Manual, RAM, Inc., Pensacola, Fla.; at local bookstores; or at our website: www
.ramministry.org.

9. Dr. Robert A. Morey, *The Origins and Teachings of Freemasonry* (Southbridge,
Mass.: Crowne Publications, 1990), 71.

10. Ibid., 35.

11. Albert Pike, *Morals and Dogma of the Ancient and Accepted Scottish Rite
of Freemasonry*, 3° Master (1871), www.illuminati-news.com/e-books/morals-
dogma/apikeintro.html.

12. Morey, 3.

13. Ibid., 36.

14. Ibid., 35, 39.

15. Albert Pike, "Instructions to the 23 Supreme Councils of the World" (14 July
1889), recorded by A. C. De La Rive in La Femme et l'Enfant dans la Francmacon-
nerie Universelle, www.geocities.com/endtimedeception/worship.htm.

Chapter 8: Satanic Ritual Abuse and Multiple Personality Disorder

1. *Satanic abuse*: The Sidran Institute (www.sidran.org) defines this as abuse
that evokes the name, image or concept of Satan as part of the abuse. Even
though this term is used interchangeably with ritual and sadistic abuse, each
has a specific meaning. Abuse could be ritual and sadistic but not satanic if the
concept of Satan is not used as a part of the abuse.

Ritual abuse: This term has been defined in a variety of ways by different
authors and researchers. One definition developed for a study on abuse in child
daycare defined ritual abuse as "abuse that occurs in a context linked to some
symbol or group activity that have a religious, magical, or supernatural connota-
tion and where the invocation of these symbols or activities, repeated over time,
is used to frighten and intimidate the children." See David Finkelhor, and Linda
Meyer Williams, *Nursery Crimes: Sexual Abuse in Day Care* (Thousand Oaks, Calif.:
Sage Publications, 1988), 59.

Another definition, developed by the Los Angeles County Commission for
Women (1989), refers to ritual abuse as, "a brutal form of abuse of children, ado-
lescents, and adults, consisting of physical, sexual, and psychological abuse, and
involving the use of rituals. Ritual does not necessarily mean satanic. However,
most survivors state that they were ritually abused as part of satanic worship
for the purpose of indoctrinating them into satanic beliefs and practices. Ritual
abuse rarely consists of a single episode. It usually involves repeated abuse
over an extended period of time." A later report in 1991 noted that there is
tremendous controversy about the objective reality of ritual abuse. While some
clinicians, researchers and police believe that ritual abuse occurs, others do not.
They believe that reports of ritual abuse are part of mass hysteria fed by media
accounts and talk show programs. There is no consensus about the reality and/or
extent of ritual abuse.

2. *Multiple Personality Disorder (MPD)*: In *DSM-III-R* (*Diagnostic and Statistical
Manual of Mental Disorders, Third Edition, Revised*), MPD is classified as a dissociative disorder. The diagnostic criteria are: The existence of two or more distinct
personalities or personality states within one person with each personality hav-

ing a distinct and consistent pattern of relating to self and the environment. At least two of these personalities or personality states recurrently take full control of the person's behavior. In general, individuals with MPD have a background of child abuse or other forms of severe childhood trauma. Dissociative identity disorder (DID) is the current name for this disorder in *DSM-IV* (*Diagnostic and Statistical Manual of Mental Disorders, Fourth Edition*).

3. Barna Research Online, "Americans Draw Theological Beliefs from Diverse Points of View" (8 October 2002), www.barna.org.

4. *Alter*: Another term for personality, alternate personality or personality state; also called an identity or dissociated part. A distinct identity or personality state, with its own relatively enduring pattern of perceiving, relating to, and thinking about the environment and self. Modified from *DSM–IV*, p. 770: "Alters are dissociated parts of the mind that the patient experiences as separate from each other." See *ISSD Practice Guidelines Glossary* (Northbrook, Ill.: International Society for the Study of Dissociation, 1994), www.issd.org.

5. *Programming*: This is a form of mind control best described as brainwashing or training done through hypnosis and torture. It involves the fragmentation of the mind by the abusers. The purpose of programming is to gain total control and loyalty of the individual.

6. James G. Friesen, Ph.D., *Uncovering the Mystery of MPD* (Eugene, Ore.: Wipf and Stock, 1991), 133.

7. *Dissociation*: The Sidran Institute describes this as the separation of ideas, feelings, information, identity or memories that would normally go together. Dissociation exists on a continuum: At one end are mild dissociative experiences common to most people (such as daydreaming or highway hypnosis) and at the other extreme is severe chronic dissociation, such as DID (MPD). Dissociation appears to be a normal process used to handle trauma that over time becomes reinforced and develops into maladaptive coping.

8. This scenario is based on actual testimonies of victims/survivors.

9. *Host*: This is the core personality, the person's original God-given personality, the true personality. It is the personality that the other personalities split away from during abuse and trauma.

10. *Dissociative identity disorder (DID)*: According to the *DSM–IV* (p. 487) there are four diagnostic criteria:

- The presence of two or more distinct identities or personality states
- At least two of these identities or personality states recurrently take control of the person's behavior
- Inability to recall important information that is too extensive to be explained by ordinary forgetfulness
- The disturbance is not due to direct physiological effects of a substance or a general medical condition.

DID is the current name for multiple personality disorder (first used in *DSM–IV*). In addition to the name change, the criteria were increased by two items—3 and 4 (see bullet points above). The term DID is felt to reflect more accurately the condition of an individual with two or more personality states. This change recognizes that MPD represents the failure to form one core personality rather than to simply create many personalities.

11. Based on actual testimonies of victims/survivors.

12. See note 6. I first read Friesen's book when I began dealing with MPD in 1998. It was the basis and the starting point for our ministry to SRA/MPD victims and survivors.

13. Much of the information in the *Deliverance Training Manual* is included in this book. For more information, please visit our website at www.ramministry .org.

14. *Borderline personality disorder (BPD)*: This is best understood as an attachment disorder. "The essential feature for Borderline Personality Disorder is a pervasive pattern or instability of interpersonal relationships, self-image, and affects, and marked impulsiveness that begins by early adulthood and is present in a variety of contexts," as indicated by five or more of the following:

- Frantic efforts to avoid real or imagined abandonment
- A pattern of unstable and intense interpersonal relationships characterized by alternating between extremes of idealization and devaluation
- Identity disturbance: marked and persistently unstable self-image or sense of self
- Impulsivity in at least two areas that are potentially self-damaging
- Recurrent suicidal behavior, gestures or threats, or self-mutilating behavior
- Affective instability due to a marked reactivity of mood
- Chronic feelings of emptiness
- Inappropriate, intense anger or difficulty controlling anger
- Transient, stress-related paranoid ideation or severe dissociative symptoms

In borderline personality disorder, like DID (MPD), there is a likelihood of a trauma history: "Physical and sexual abuse, neglect, hostile conflict, and early parental loss or separation are more common in the childhood histories of those with Borderline Personality Disorder." This information was adapted from *DSM–IV* (pp. 650–54) of the International Society for the Study of Dissociation and the Sidran Institute's Trauma Disorders Glossary.

15. *Regression*: The return to earlier or younger behavior and thinking. Trauma often overwhelms everyday defenses and brings about behavioral changes. Child personality states are an example of trauma-based regression. In "age regression," a person experiences himself or herself at a specific earlier age. The person does not always return to the age of a child, however. Age regression may take a client back just a few years earlier in adult life.

16. *Flashbacks*: A type of spontaneous abreaction common to victims of acute trauma. Also known as "intrusive recall," flashbacks have been categorized into four types: dreams or nightmares; dreams from which the dreamer awakens but remains under the influence of the dream content and has difficulty making contact with reality; conscious flashbacks in which a person "relives" a traumatic event with no awareness at that time; or later, of the connection between the

flashback and the past trauma. See Frank W. Putnam, *Diagnosis and Treatment of Multiple Personality Disorder* (New York: Putnam), 236–37.

17. *Body memory*: Lenore Terr, M.D., gave me this explanation. This popularly used term is actually a misnomer. The body does not have neurons capable of remembering; only the brain does. The term refers to body sensations that symbolically or literally capture some aspect of trauma. Sensory impulses are recorded in the parietal lobes of the brain, and these remembrances of bodily sensations can be felt when similar occurrences or cues restimulate the stored memories. The Sidran Institute notes further that this type of bodily sensation may occur in any sensory mode: tactile, taste, smell, kinesthetic or sight. A person who was raped, for instance, may later experience pelvic pain similar to that experience at the time of the event. Body memories may be diagnosed as somatoform disorder.

18. *Switching*: This is the process of changing from one already existing personality state or fragment to another personality state or fragment. Switching may be initiated by outside stimuli such as an environmental *trigger*, or by internal stimuli, such as feelings or memories. Switching may be observable, such as changes in posture, facial expression, changes in voice tone or speech patterns. Switching may also be observed by changes in mood, regressed behavior and variable cognitive functioning.

Trigger: An event, object, person, etc., that sets a series of thoughts in motion or reminds a person of some aspect of his or her traumatic past. The person may be unaware of what has "triggered" the memory (loud noises, a particular color, piece of music, odor). Learning not to overreact to triggers is a therapeutic task in the treatment of dissociative disorders.

19. *Inner self-helper (ISH)*: A personality state, often a helper or protector, that has knowledge of the system and works with the therapist to facilitate the treatment.

20. *Mapping*: According to the Sidran Institute this is a technique used in psychotherapy with DID (MPD) clients to gain knowledge about the internal personality system. The client is asked to draw a map or diagram of the personality states to explain the inner world of personalities. This provides useful information about the system, such as the connections or lack of connections between personality states. The map may need to be updated as therapy progresses and can be used for integration work to help ensure that all internal parts have been integrated. It is also known as personality mapping or system mapping. Mapping can be used to understand the relationships among feeling states as well.

21. *System*: This is a descriptive term used to refer to all of the parts of the mind in an individual with DID (MPD). This includes personality states, memories, feelings, ego states, entities and any other way of describing dissociated aspects of an individual. It is more helpful in treatment to consider parts of a system rather than separate personality states. Also called internal system or personality system.

22. The MPD tracking sheet is a simple spreadsheet for recording information on alters. It includes the name and age of the personality, the trauma that caused the split and the date discovered. Our sheet also records whether or not the alter is believed to be demonized, and if it was integrated to the host.

23. Informed consent: In psychotherapy, informed consent occurs when a client is informed of:

- The diagnosis
- The nature of the treatment being considered
- The risks and benefits of such treatment
- The likely outcome with and without treatment
- Alternative approaches to relieve the symptoms

The information must be presented in a form the client can understand and consent must be given without coercion. Often this information is presented in written form, which the client signs, thereby giving permission for treatment. While this has historically been common for medical procedures and psychological research, it is now also being done during psychotherapy, especially with specific techniques such as hypnosis and sodium amytal interviews. Taken from the Sidran Institute Trauma Disorders Glossary.

24. *False memory*: This is a term developed in the early 1990s by the False Memory Syndrome Foundation to describe "memories" that are not based on actual events. This is different from delayed memories and repressed memories.

25. B. A. Robinson, "MPD/DID Seen as a Psychological Disorder," Ontario Consultants on Religious Tolerance, January 11, 1998, www.religioustolerance .org/mpd_did3.htm.

Chapter 9: Emotional Wounding

1. Bob and Shirley Johnson presented this list at a Cleansing Stream seminar. Their talk was entitled "Healing the Wounded Spirit."

2. See the fact sheet at the National Institute of Mental Health website: www .nimh.nih.gov/publicat/numbers.cfm.

3. Connie S. Chan, Ph.D, *If It Runs in Your Family: Depression* (New York: Bantam, 1993), 4.

4. Bob and Shirley Johnson presented this statistic from the book *Secret Life of the Unborn Child* by Thomas Verny, M.D. (New York: Dell, 1994).

5. Ibid.

6. Doris Wagner, *How to Cast Out Demons: A Beginner's Guide* (Colorado Springs: Wagner Institute for Practical Ministry, 1999).

7. Jack Hayford explained this phenomenon in a talk entitled "Cleansing, Liberty and Maturity," given at a Cleansing Stream Ministries seminar in 1997.

8. This was a further talk by Jack Hayford entitled "Sanctification: Key to Overcoming Confusion."

9. Joyce Meyer, *The Root of Reaction* (Tulsa: Harrison House, 1994), 25.

10. David A. Seamands, *Healing for Damaged Emotions* (Colorado Springs: Chariot Victor, 1991), 49.

11. Ibid., 53.

12. Ibid., 25–6.

13. Meyer, 97.

Chapter 10: The Basis for Ministry

1. I am grateful to Timothy Davis for pointing out these specific needs within the Body in a talk entitled, "Confess Your Sins," given at a Cleansing Stream Ministries seminar, Van Nuys, Calif., 1997.

Chapter 12: Why People Do Not Get Free

1. John Bevere, *The Bait of Satan* (Lake Mary, Fla.: Creation House, 1997), 112.

2. Ibid., 13.

3. Ibid., 138.

Index

William Sudduth is founder and president of Righteous Acts Ministries. He is formerly a member of the pastoral staff and head of the deliverance ministry teams at Brownsville Revival School of Ministry (Pensacola, Fla.) He was also a member of the faculty teaching classes on spiritual warfare. He travels nationally and internationally, ministering in seminars, retreats and training sessions on the subjects of deliverance and inner healing.

Bill is the author of three books, *So Free! An In-Depth Guide to Deliverance and Inner Healing; Deliverance Training Manual;* and *What's Behind the Ink? The Spiritual Aspects of Tattoos, Piercing and Other Fads.* Bill is a member of the Founder's Circle of the International Society of Deliverance Ministers (ISDM), directed by Peter and Doris Wagner. He oversees other ministers and ministries as the apostolic leader of the Apostolic Association of Related Ministers (AARM) and is a faculty member at Wagner Leadership Institute.

During the last eight years Bill has led more than a thousand individual deliverance sessions and has ministered to thousands of people as a seminar instructor. To date, he has trained hundreds of ministers in the areas of deliverance and inner healing and continues to do so through regularly scheduled local and regional deliverance training seminars.

Bill's vision is to bring revival to the Church through restoration; to see the Body of Christ become a pure, spotless, holy Bride, ready for the soon return of our Lord Jesus Christ; to bring healing and deliverance to the Church; and to equip the saints to do the work of the ministry.

Bill and his wife, Janet, have three children and two grand-children and live in Fort Walton Beach, Florida.

For further information, or to be in touch with Bill Sudduth, contact:

RAM (Righteous Acts Ministries)
P.O. Box 1141
Fort Walton Beach, FL 32549
Phone: (850) 390-4104
website: www.ramministry.org
e-mail: office@ramministry.org